Much *More* than a JOB

than a JOB

Your 24 / 7 Mission

by Dr. W. Paul "Buddy" Crum, Jr.

Bridge-Logos
Orlando, Florida 32822

Bridge-Logos

Orlando, FL 32822 USA

Much More than a Job
by Dr. W. Paul "Buddy" Crum, Jr.

Library of Congress Catalog Card Number: 2006931581
International Standard Book Number 0-88270-232-7

G163.316.N.m607.35240

Contents

Bringing Down the Walls

I had a dramatic encounter with Jesus Christ when I was fifteen. Earlier, at the age of eight, I had been baptized in a Baptist church, but my new experience with Jesus as a teenager far exceeded that of my baptism. Even so, my encounter with the Lord added an area of confusion and frustration to my teenage mind as I thought about my future career. I wanted very much to serve the Lord, for I had been taught that full-time ministry was a higher or greater calling than any other. This teaching led me to believe that serving God involved being paid directly for full-time ministry and was probably only available in the church or on the mission field.

However, my mother had encouraged me to become an orthodontist. There wasn't one in our small town so she had taken my two sisters to the closest one, which was forty-five miles away. Mother knew that there was a need and a demand for a local orthodontist. Such a career would keep me at my home, and it would mean that I would not be working for my father, the businessman. I greatly respected my mother and I wanted to please her. I also wanted to please and serve God. But my heart's desire was to be a businessman. Through the years I have discovered that many people have had to face a similar dilemma, especially those who have had a deep personal experience with the Lord. How was I to choose? I had to make a decision.

I decided to enroll at Emory University in Atlanta, Georgia, and take the required sciences to pursue a career as an orthodontist. In my heart, though, I still desired to be in business school. I remained frustrated until I finally confessed to my mother I really did not want to be an orthodontist. She, in turn, supported my decision to begin studying the principles of business, even though I was well on my way to a degree in biology.

Eventually I entered the business world as a very ambitious entrepreneur. My intention, as was the case with most things I attempted, was to make a great deal of money and give large amounts to the church after I was blessed. I did not, however, understand God's principles of tithing and giving at this point in my life.

Then I read a book on the life of R.J. LeTourneau, a successful entrepreneur. His life's goal was to be a giver, so he continually increased his giving until he was ultimately giving ninety percent of his income. I began to see this as a vital principle in God's plan and began tithing. After college, I was married to my devoted wife, Mary.

As the years passed, I desired a greater understanding of how to become a more effective business person. While continuing to work and attending graduate school, I began to take great risks, many of which turned out to be successful. During this time I was beginning to establish and distinguish myself in the financial services industry and as a Christian layman.

I enjoyed the challenges of business, and I enjoyed taking risks. By the time I was fifty I had tasted success four times and had experienced failure four times. Because of my strong ambition, I developed into a very hard, driving person. I was not very sensitive to other people's needs even though I thought I was, especially if they were not performing up to my expectations. I had made the same judgments that most business people tend to make—the Church was not that relevant to business.

I can remember times when I would sit in church and think, "That would work in biblical times but not in today's fast-changing environment." The main function of a Christian layman seemed to me to be that of a giver. God would bless you if you gave generously and didn't sin, especially by committing "the big ones." If you did happen to sin, though, I knew you needed to receive forgiveness. Of course, you were to treat other people in the church with respect, as well. Also, if you were put in a position to witness to someone about Christ, you were to do so. That, in a nutshell, was my view of Christianity.

God Changed My Agenda!

Mary and I grew in our relationship with each other and with the Lord. We were faithful church members, and I became an elder in our local church. I even served on a number of large ministry boards. My wife and I had raised our level of giving to over thirty percent of our income by increasing it by one percent per year. Things seemed to be going well; however, something was going on within me during this period of my life. I had a deep sense of unrest in my spirit, and I thought it was time for me to take another big business risk.

One day, as I was entering my office, I heard a voice that stopped me in my tracks. It said, *"You don't need to own anything else."* By this time I had learned to rebuke the devil, which I promptly did. As I sat down at my desk, the voice said the same thing to me again. This time I was shocked. I was at a time in my life when I owned quite a bit but I felt I could definitely stand to own more. I did not listen to the voice I'd heard and so I began a new aggressive venture. Here I was at age forty-eight, with much business experience, and plenty of capital. I was highly educated and I had good business contacts. But, as time went on, I lost a great deal of money on that aggressive business venture. After this great disappointment and financial reversal I was really "set up" for what was to happen next.

Later, as I reflected on this dramatic experience, I realized the Lord was indeed "setting me up," but He was also protecting me. I learned a great lesson from that experience, which will become clear to you as you read through this book. Stated simply, the lesson was this: God did not withdraw His love, mercy, and grace from me personally or from my family. He did, however, withdraw His grace or anointing from the business portion of my life.

At the age of forty-eight, God drastically changed my life's agenda. God called Mary and me in a very dramatic way to start a church, a new type of church —a prophetic church. God was again dramatically changing everything: my doctrines, my agendas, my relationships, and my direction. I thought, "Why now, God? And another thing, you know I don't like the retail business!" To me, what was happening felt more like an interruption than a life's call. As entrepreneurial as I had been, this new venture had not been on my life's radar screen. After all, I still had to prove some things to the world and to myself concerning my business ability. At the same time, though, I knew I had to listen to the voice of the Lord.

I am so thankful for my wife and for her wisdom and her ability to hear and follow God. To be sure, Mary was much more excited about this whole thing than I was! She confidently confirmed that God was calling us, so we began this journey despite my confusion. Her enthusiasm propelled us forward into a full-time pulpit ministry.

Throughout our pulpit ministry, I have gained a much deeper understanding of ministry in general, including local church dynamics. I had always liked people, and I enjoyed selling to them. But pastoring people was not my forte. As we began this journey together, I asked God to give me a pastor's heart. Now I know He has been faithful in answering that prayer.

Biblical Principles for the Marketplace

During my time in the marketplace, I gained a very broad and rich understanding of business, especially with regard to marketing. I had no idea that God was going to use this training and experience directly within the Body of Christ, however.

Now, as a pastor, I began to see hard-working and often ambitious church people being challenged by their businesses. From my deep experience in the marketplace, I understood how to build a business, so I began to teach the principles of business success to others in the church family. This led to a personal desire to understand the foundational, biblical principles about business. As these principles were revealed to me, I began writing and teaching about seven distinct, foundational principles. Certainly, there are more principles than these seven, but these are truly essential.

In cooperation and association with Dr. Bill Hamon, Founder and Director of Christian International, along with several other business people who had a similar desire for Marketplace Ministry, firm foundational resources were made available. Adding to these resources, I wrote *Ministry to the Marketplace*. Later, I founded the Marketplace Alliance and the Marketplace Alliance School. All of this has led me to compile the core of my ministry—what I call *Marketplace Ministry*. The principles of Marketplace Ministry are simply stated as:

1. VISION
2. PLANNING
3. WORKMANSHIP
4. STEWARDSHIP
5. SERVANTHOOD
6. ETHICS and INTEGRITY
7. HEARING GOD

Underlying all of these principles is the foundational principle of God himself—LOVE.

As you read this book, you will discover how to work in the marketplace in such a way that God's kingdom will be advanced, and you will become the agent of vision and change that God has created you to be. Join me in this incredible journey into the vital and exciting concept of Marketplace Ministry.

CHAPTER 1

What is Marketplace Ministry?

S tudying the parables, we discover that Jesus gave instructions to His disciples and other followers concerning their gifts and talents. Having different talents in varying degrees, each person was expected to take responsibility for those talents in order to produce results. They were expected to find ways to *increase* that which they had been given.

In Matthew 25, we see that the Parable of the Talents is actually about responsibility. The owner greatly rewarded his two stewards who doubled the principle of their talents. The word "talent" here is referring to money, commerce, and business. In response to the servant who had been given one talent, which he buried, the master punished him because of his lack of planning and production. He had simply failed to *take responsibility*. Salvation or being born again should be the beginning, not the end, of our redemptive life. Like the servants in this parable, marketplace people will be held accountable for their use of any gifts and talents God has given to them.

In speaking at conferences, I often remind business people in the audience that there are two judgments. The first judgment is the Great White Throne Judgment. This judgment is reserved for those who are represented by wheat and tares, the sheep and goats, or the saved and unsaved. If they have accepted Christ as their personal Savior, they will pass through that judgment.

Once the separation is made, members of the Body of Christ will face another judgment. This judgment takes place at the Judgment Seat of Christ. Here we will each be judged for our actions while on earth, including those that took place in the marketplace. The more dedicated ones will say to Christ, "Lord, I was faithful in my church. I attended Sunday school and I even went to church on Wednesday evenings. Oh, and I also was a giver in my church." The Lord will commend you for your faithfulness, but then He will quickly remind you that those works were for your benefit.

While there are many good works that take place in and through individual congregations, the local church should be your training ground. God gave the local church to you in order to train and equip you, to build you up, and to make you strong so you will be able to fulfill your calling in your personal sphere of influence.

Ultimately, your calling is not to the local church but to the marketplace!

The Church should be the most powerful and most influential organization on the earth. It has the greatest distribution system, as well as the most assets in terms of materials and people. But the Church is not acknowledged in political or business decisions because it is so fragmented. We have allowed our doctrines to become points of great separation, and this fragmentation has lessened our effectiveness in bringing about change on the earth.

Dualism is prevalent in the minds of most Christians today because they do not understand the importance of their future marketplace assignments and their calling to the Body of Christ. Most people are not fulfilled, especially in their spiritual lives, because they have not found their spiritual purpose. I will elaborate more on this later. For now, be aware of the fragmentation that exists in the Church today due to this lack of understanding and unity.

We need to come to the realization that the true purpose of the local church should be to equip and empower the saints for effective living in all areas of their lives, especially beyond the church walls. This should be our ultimate goal rather than getting people saved just to teach them parts of the Bible, basically leaving them non-effective in their sphere of influence outside the church walls where God wants to use them.

If we could all agree on some of the basic principles of the Bible, this would enable us to become, as the Apostle Paul taught so frequently, unified. Unity does not denote being the same. It speaks of agreement that is built on biblical principles. We need to be unified so that we can become the effective and powerful organization we were designed to be, even in the marketplace.

Marketplace Ministry

The original and ongoing plan and move of God that we must enter into today is that He is restoring things to the original mandate which He gave to the first man and woman in the Garden of Eden (the first marketplace). There were three direct commands that were given to them concerning His master plan. One was to be fruitful; two was to multiply—I believe this means that they were to multiply both naturally and spiritually; and three was to take dominion or rulership over all of His creation. (See Gen. 1:28.)

To fulfill God's original mandate, it will require the Church to become unified and be without walls or limitations. This will be a Church that sets people free and prepares them to take dominion in the marketplace, the place where they have a sphere of influence. This sphere of influence is where they have been assigned by the Holy Spirit to make a difference in our world.

This sphere of influence includes the four basics of any society: religion, government, family, and commerce. *This is the concept of*

Marketplace Ministry. As Christians, you and I are called to be change agents, to be both salt and light. We have been strategically positioned to bring down the functional walls of separation in our specific marketplace.

Why the Marketplace?

The marketplace is quite simply where the majority of the people spend the majority of their time. This is where most saved men and women spend a large percentage of their daily working time interacting with the majority of the world's lost population. This has been referred to as the "9-to-5 window." Statistics show that only two percent of the local church population will be in pulpit ministry or employed on a church staff. Therefore, we know that the vast majority of the population is functioning most of the time within the marketplace. The marketplace is a strategic location when it comes to the daily affairs of people. Interactions and activities there can be as simple as a mother buying a gallon of milk at a grocery store, or as complex as a multi-billion dollar business transaction between industry giants.

The marketplace is also the proving ground for what we believe and who we are. It is the place where ideas are exchanged, concepts are tried, and values are clearly demonstrated. God's move in the marketplace is not by chance, but by design.

The marketplace, therefore, is about kingdom business, and kingdom business is about evangelism, missions, successful business principles and practices, the integration of work and faith, economic development, spreading the gospel, transforming nations, and transforming lives. It is a combination of all of these.

Paul recognized the importance of proclaiming the gospel in the *marketplace.* We read in Acts 17:17, "Therefore he reasoned in the synagogue with the Jews and with the Gentile worshipers, and in the marketplace daily with those who happened to be there." The Greek word translated as "marketplace" in this text is *agora.* The *agora* was "a large open space, often found near the gates of cities in New Testament times, where goods were bought and sold. The *agora* was also the site for public assemblies. While in Athens, the apostle Paul shared his faith with people in the agora." *

The vast majority of Christians are called to a Marketplace Ministry! You may prefer to think of this calling in terms of a *workplace ministry*. Either way, it is all part of God's ongoing, full-time, master plan. Let me challenge you to consider that there are no part-time Christians. Every one of us has a vocation—a calling. We are on call, and we are accountable to God and to one another on a 24/7 basis. You and I are not part-time workers, but we are full-time Christians. Christian physicians are simply messengers of Christ disguised as doctors. A Christian banker is simply a servant of Jesus Christ who is on assignment as a banker. The same is true for Christian tradesmen, professionals, "techies," blue-collar employees, and workers in every other industry on the face of the earth.

You may be wrapped up in a garment of some trade, but at the same time, be a representative of Christ wherever you are. You might say, "I am a salesman and I go to church." Though this is true, you need to take it a step further by saying, "I am a salesman for the Kingdom of God," one who has a product or service to sell that gives you a marketplace platform or pulpit.

We read about two tax collectors who were saved in the New Testament—Matthew and Zacchaeus. Early in His ministry, Jesus called Matthew to follow Him as a disciple. However, He instructed Zacchaeus to continue to be a tax collector, but to be a righteous and just worker in the Kingdom of God instead of unjustly robbing people, as was the practice in the Roman world in those days.

Whether you are an accountant, a teacher, a housewife, a lawyer, or an executive in your trade, your eternal purpose is for the Kingdom

---

* (*Nelson's Illustrated Bible Dictionary*, Thomas Nelson Publishers, 1986)

of God. Wherever God has placed you, that is where you are to serve Him, and that is where you will be held accountable. Christ has a plan and purpose for you wherever you are.

Read Acts 16:16-34. Just as Paul and Silas used their time in prison as a marketplace platform, you and I carry Christ within us wherever we go. Remember, you are *always* a believer; therefore, you are *always* a witness for Christ.

Seasons of Growth for the Church

God is dynamic; therefore, His plan for His Kingdom is also dynamic or active. Just as there are seasons of growth in the natural, there are specific seasons of growth in the Church as well.

Each season has a timing, a purpose, and an active work to be completed. *In this season_you are in, God has you right where He wants you—as an instrument in His Kingdom plan for the Church.* The season of work you are in right now should be filled with God's purpose! "To everything there is a season, a time for every purpose under heaven" (Eccles. 3:1). Read further in Ecclesiastes to learn how the purpose, the season, and the work you are to do are all interconnected in the Lord's master plan.

> *"What profit has the worker from that in which he labors? I have seen the God-given task with which the sons of men are to be occupied. He has made everything beautiful in its time. Also He has put eternity in their hearts, except that no one can find out the work that God does from beginning to end.*

> *"I know that nothing is better for them than to rejoice, and to do good in their lives, and also that every man should eat and drink and enjoy the good of all his labor—it is the gift of God.*

"I know that whatever God does, it shall be forever. Nothing can be added to it, and nothing taken from it. God does it, that men should fear before Him. That which is has already been, and what is to be has already been; and God requires an account of what is past" (Eccles. 3:9-15).

The Scriptures makes it clear that there are different seasons for different reasons. The Church has already come through many seasons; each was unique in itself. We call these seasons "moves of God." Each season or move of God takes the Church to a higher level of wisdom, knowledge, understanding, and impact. This is so mankind can begin to know and function in the purposes of God and can be brought closer to the final phases of the master plan.

A very small difference exists between societies, such as cities, where there are many churches with large congregations and other areas with fewer churches and lower attendance. Many surveys and articles show how churchgoers and the unchurched have the same problems, divorce rates, financial difficulties, social problems, poverty, crime rates, etc. The church has made little impact on society or culture. This should not be the case. This is a result of dualism and the lack of impact of the Church upon society.

Martin Luther became a revolutionary leader of the Protestant Reformation when he nailed his "95 Theses" to the door of the Castle Church in Wittenberg, Germany, on October 31, 1517. This season saw a dramatic change in the structure of the Church.

The purpose was to establish the "Priesthood of Believers." This movement became instrumental in helping Christians understand the "institution of work" as being part of God's plan for each person to live by faith, and it showed how believers are justified by faith. This revelation greatly differed from the Greek and Roman teachings of the previous season.

Luther's revelation was rooted in Romans 5:1, and it reinforced the truth that people had direct access to God through Jesus Christ. In other words, Christians came to realize it was not necessary to go through another person, such as a priest, to have access to the Father. This move of God revealed that Christians can go directly to the throne of grace through prayer in the name of Jesus Christ. As a matter of fact, Christians learned that we are invited to enter God's throne room, the Holy of Holies, boldly and confidently. This teaching helps us see that every believer has a ministry. Therefore, the Reformation reinforced the concept of the "ministry of all believers."

The Apostolic Reformation

Once this move of God began to gain momentum, many denominations and mainline churches rose up, each identifying specific areas of Scripture on which they established their doctrinal interpretations. As time evolved, these doctrinal interpretations became denominations that had good intentions and results, but eventually separated the Church and its people.

Thankfully, a new move of God, referred to as the *Apostolic Reformation* is now taking place. This season will lead us to the *Saints' Movement*, in which believers will do the work of the ministry wherever they are positioned. This is what I mean by *Marketplace Ministry*. The Apostle Paul explained this purpose in Ephesians 4:11-12:

> *"And He Himself gave some to be apostles, some prophets, some evangelists, and some pastors and teachers, for the equipping of the saints for the work of ministry, for the edifying of the body of Christ."*

Unfortunately, the United States is not experiencing this apostolic move as strongly as other countries around the world are. For example, in Nigeria there are churches with over one million members. This phenomenon began when one drug dealer was saved on the streets. He immediately began evangelizing and preaching to other drug dealers.

As they were converted and then trained, they began to use their God-given marketing talents to advance the Kingdom of God on those same streets. In reality, the talents were already there, but they had been perverted. This one man's mission was to take the drug dealers around him away from the kingdom of darkness and lead them into the Kingdom of Light. After receiving Christ, they, too, began using their giftings as business people to make money for the Kingdom of God. This allowed for the large expansion of the church in areas of both finances and witnessing in that whole country.

In Seoul, Korea, Pastor David Yonggi Cho pastors one of the largest churches in the world today. His conversion also happened on the street, so a great part of his ministry has taken place on the streets of Seoul. These men are vivid examples of true redemption and restoration in the Church today.

Knowing What to Do

You and I can no longer claim ignorance about what God wants us to do in bringing unity to the Body of Christ! The Apostolic Reformation is perfectly described and clarified for us in the Book of Ephesians. Paul's letter to the Ephesian believers was written for the purpose of bringing reconciliation and unity among the believers in order to establish God's kingdom here on the earth. Paul based his instructions on what Jesus had declared in His prayer that is recorded in Matthew 6:10: *"Thy kingdom come. Thy will be done in earth, as it is in heaven" (KJV).*

This revelation of God's plan for the Church is evident when Paul speaks of the reconciliation of all believers, in all areas of their relationships—Jews and Gentiles, husbands and wives, parents and children, as well as employers and employees.

The Apostle Paul tells us that God, *"... hath put all things under his [Christ's] feet, and gave him to be the head over all things to the his body, the fulness of him that filleth all in all" (Eph.*

He then teaches us that it is by grace, which is God's divine enablement, that we are saved through faith. (See Eph. 2:8-9.) Paul makes it clear that salvation is a gift of God; it cannot be earned through works.

This explanation is immediately followed by the explanation that there were, however, works that were created before the foundation of the world, works that were designed for each believer to do or accomplish. All these works were specifically designed to be accomplished in the marketplace. Paul says that we are to "walk in them:" *"For we are his workmanship, created in Christ Jesus unto good works, which God hath before ordained that we should walk in them" (Eph. 2:10, KJV).*

All of this confirms that you were predestined in the mind of God—before creation or we could say in eternity past. You existed in eternity past with God before creation. Before time was, you were. This shows us that creation precedes formation. In other words, you were created before you were formed. (Read Eph. 1:4-12, which reveals that God chose you before the foundation of the world.) God has now placed your spirit in a natural vessel which is called "the flesh," and He has breathed His life into you, equipped you with talents and giftings, and given you a calling that is based upon His preordained works that He expects you to do.

Essentially, this is your story:
• You were beautifully and uniquely made by God; therefore, you are special. Very special, indeed!
• You have been dispatched into time for this season in order to do good works on the earth.
• You have been given a portion of grace and faith to do the exact things that He has assigned for you to do.
• You have a special, predestined place in God's master plan with regard to the building of His Kingdom on earth.

We have all been given natural abilities by God, our heavenly Father. We are to improve or perfect these through acquired skills, but we should also remember that He has given us access to His supernatural resources and grace through faith. We are each fully equipped for the assignment we have been destined to fulfill.

Understanding the Apostolic Reformation

There are many characteristics of the *Apostolic Movement* that are too broad to define here. However, there are a few aspects that I do want to mention in order to help you understand how God is raising up a church without walls, a church that will bring about reconciliation, restoration, and the release of the saints into Marketplace Ministry.

Spiritual Fathering

The Church is now experiencing the *Restoration of Fathering*. Spiritual fathering is typified by The Elijah and Elisha Company, a contemporary ministry within the Body of Christ. Spiritual fathering refers to an approach in which those who are mature in Marketplace Ministry impart God's gifts and training into the lives of less-mature believers who need coaching, mentoring, and teaching.

This kind of fathering was prophesied in Malachi 4:6:

> *"And he will turn the hearts of the fathers to the children, and the hearts of the children to their fathers, lest I come and strike the earth with a curse."*

In the last days, the hearts of children in the faith and their spiritual fathers are being knit together. This is for the express purpose of bringing reconciliation and unity within the Body of Christ.

Many of these spiritual fathers are now active in the marketplace. They do not have to be the employers or the bosses. They may not even be in the same businesses or professions that those they are fathering are in. They are simply those who are marketplace apostles or have an apostolic anointing that will enable them to spiritually father others.

In this way mentoring and sponsorship are being developed for the purpose of bringing restoration to relationships. Most importantly, intimacy between God and man is being fostered. This is part of the renewal of material and spiritual counseling. As we are restored emotionally and holistically to the Father, God's plans and purposes for our lives are revealed.

This emphasis on fathering in the *Apostolic Reformation* has come about because many people have an "orphan spirit." They feel, and often have been, orphaned emotionally or spiritually, by their natural parents, by their educational and religious institutions, and by their business partners. Relationships that are built on biblical covenant principles are now being restored. These relationships are rooted in such biblical covenant values as integrity, honesty, trust, justice, truth, righteousness, favor, commitment, Christ-centeredness, forgiveness, love, and transparent, open communication.

Note the difference between those who are to be spiritual fathers and those who are called to be mentors. Spiritual fathers are those who speak truth and blessing into your life, are concerned for your character and spiritual maturity, and are willing to confront and encourage you in all areas of your life.

Those who are mentors are there to instruct you and support you in your career and goal development. There can be many mentors in your life, depending on the rate of your growth and advancement. This is not so with spiritual fathers. This is why the Bible says, *"For though you might have ten thousand instructors in Christ, yet you do not have many fathers" (1 Cor. 4:15).*

Fathering Revealed by Jesus

At the time of my conversion, it was really easy for me to identify with Jesus, because I knew He identified with me. He carried the cross for me, He died for me, and He forgave my sins. At times I even believed that Jesus was there to protect me from a God who could become upset with me! Later I realized that Jesus came for the purpose of showing me the Father's heart and to reveal to me how deeply and completely the Father loves me. Knowing the heart of the Father involves knowing that He desires a family upon whom He can pour His unconditional love. Obviously, Jesus and His Father are one in purpose, love, and sacrifice.

The biblical concept of family is defined as "house" or "household": the Hebrew word is *bayit*; the Greek word is *oikia*. *Bayit* and *oikia* both refer to "house, household, family, or home." These words are used in reference to ordinary dwellings, i.e. the place in which a family lives, but they also refer to a corporate group or family of descendants.

A household is not just a nuclear family of parents and children, but it is also the aggregate of all their relatives and descendants (the extended and multigenerational family). In fact, a household speaks of an entire community of people related to one another not only by birth but also by commerce, interactions, faith, and caring relationships. In a spiritual sense and as a transforming truth, the marketplace becomes a household or family in which God acts to advance His Kingdom through these family relationships. (Read Gen. 18:19; 35:2; Josh. 24:14; 2 Sam. 7:4-16; Matt. 10:11-14; John 4:46-54; Acts 10:1-14, 11:1-14, 16:11-15; 16:25-34; 18:7-8; 1 Cor. 1:14-16; Heb. 11:7.)

The Father had no way of fully demonstrating His unconditional love to us, His family, until He sent Jesus. He gave us a dramatic demonstration of the truth that no greater love exists than that which is shown when a man lays down his life for his brothers. God had to come in the form of man, Jesus, to demonstrate the extent of His love to mankind. The Kingdom of God on earth will advance to a new level as soon as the hearts of the fathers are restored to the sons and the hearts of the sons are turned back to their fathers. Spiritual fathers are needed to father, mentor, and train the sons for the work of the ministry, especially in the marketplace.

Five-Fold Ministry

Jesus was raised in the marketplace as king, priest, and prophet; He was not raised in the Temple, although He was faithful in attending services there. He spent the first thirty years of His life being prepared for and functioning in the trade of carpentry. Since He was the oldest son, He probably ran the carpentry shop after Joseph died. Jesus did much of His earthly ministry in the workplace. After completing His work on earth, Jesus ascended on high to give gifts to His Body, gifts which would continue His ministry to the saints. He gave these gifts so the saints/believers would be matured and equipped to do the work of the Kingdom. The Holy Spirit was then sent to indwell the believer and bring heaven's assignments, and to counsel and empower the saints.

As part of this movement, Jesus has given specific gifts to His body, the Church, for the purpose of preparing the saints or believers to complete these assignments. These gifts are listed in Ephesians 4:11: apostles, prophets, evangelists, pastors, and teachers, and these ministry gifts are usually referred to as the Five-Fold Ministry. We need all of these gifts functioning within the Body of Christ in order to complete our mission on earth.

Jesus instructed us to go and make disciples of all nations. This Great Commission cannot take place fully inside the four walls of a local church. We need to be outside the walls of the church, where the people are—in the marketplace. More than 70 percent of the Body of Christ functions in the work force (and in the marketplace) on a regular basis but does not effectively demonstrate the power of the Kingdom in their everyday lives. Why aren't they doing so? They need to know that they are equipped and empowered to be able to go forth and do everything God wants them to do. Of vital importance to utilizing this divine empowerment that is available to them is employing God's power principles and building according to His vision.

Today, as part of the *Apostolic Move of God*, we are beginning to experience the equipping and empowering of the saints to do the work of the ministry as Paul mentioned in Ephesians 4:11-13. It's important for us to realize that this is not speaking of ministry in local church settings only. Remember that the local church is to be the training ground. The fact is, though, that we have to *want* to be trained. Once we know we have a ministry call from God, the next step becomes our choice. Jesus often asked those who were seeking healing, "Do you want to get well?" Perhaps He asking us now, "Do you *want* to be trained, equipped, and empowered? Do you *want* to be part of this Apostolic Move of God?"

From a Local Church Perspective to a Kingdom View

It is important to realize that the purpose of the local church goes well beyond people receiving Christ, being baptized, and being filled with the Holy Spirit. Of course these are necessary beginning steps, but the ultimate purpose of the local church should be to provide a place where believers learn, practice, and are perfected for the work of the Kingdom.

The local church, then, should be the place where we are to…

- Teach
- Equip
- Train
- Inspire
- Mature
- Empower
- Heal—physically, emotionally, and spiritually
- Comfort

God is asking you today if you want to be part of this movement in His Church. Do you want to fulfill your future and purpose within God's Kingdom plan? The apostles in the early church were the *sent ones*. They went to new regions to establish churches, release evangelists, and establish policies and spiritual government. This concept of being sent also involves believers being sent into the marketplace as mentors or spiritual fathers.

We may also see changes in the functions of the other five-fold ministry gifts. The preparing of the saints for the work of the Kingdom may now include the teaching of such marketplace principles and skills as how to start a new business, how to build wealth for the Kingdom of God, and how to use the gifts in your work place. Church services will, therefore, have to move from being held just on Sundays in a church building to being held in office buildings on a daily basis or even several times a day. I understand that it may be hard to comprehend all this when you consider your current work place setting, but change is coming.

The local church will have to move toward becoming more effective at equipping and training the saints for this Marketplace Ministry. This means that there will be a distinct change from the ministry style in which we see one person doing everything to a team of gifted people working together.

Just as there are those on a church staff who are music ministers, singles ministers, youth and children's ministers, the most effective team will also include Marketplace Ministers who will support and train those who are specifically in a business or a profession for the work of ministry in the marketplace.

First, we must understand that God has a strategic plan for all His creation, including you and me. He is 100 percent for our success, so He has provided all the resources we will ever need, including the restoration of our relationship with Him through Jesus Christ. In order to apprehend the fullness of His promises and provisions, it is necessary to understand and operate our lives according to His principles.

Fundamentally, many of these principles or laws were given to Moses by God, and they are recorded in the Book of Deuteronomy. In the New Testament these principles were expanded upon and demonstrated by Jesus through His life and teachings. These same principles were also part of the fabric of the founding of America and the writing of the U.S. Constitution. As we move into studying Marketplace Ministry, I believe there are "Seven Biblical Principles" that are essential for our success.

I want to delineate briefly the relationship between laws and principles. "Biblical law is an orderly system of rules and regulations by which a society is governed. In the Bible, particularly the Old Testament, a unique law code was established by direct revelation from God to direct His people in their worship, in their relationship to Him, and in their social relationships with one another" (From *Nelson's Illustrated Bible Dictionary*, Copyright (c) 1986, Thomas Nelson Publishers).

Principles are "the elements, or rudiments, of any art, science, or discipline." (The Greek word is *stoicheion*—see Heb 5:12). In Hebrews 6:1 (KJV) the word "principles" (in Greek the word is *arche*) refers to the fundamentals of the doctrine of Christ. The New American Standard Version provides us with this translation: "elementary teaching," and the New International Version uses the phrases, "elementary truths" and "elementary teachings," respectively. *

Marketplace Ministry is built on truths, laws, and principles. We base these principles on God's Word, knowing they are mandates, not suggestions. Laws are specific commands, while principles are foundational truths which weave these commands through the whole of Scripture. These principles are essential for us to implement ministry

---

* (This material is adapted from *The New Unger's Bible Dictionary*, 1988.)

and penetrate our culture as salt and light in the marketplace. We cannot ever afford to be casual, disinterested, or lukewarm about Marketplace Ministry.

Let's see why God has chosen the marketplace as a primary sphere of mission and then proceed to uncover the necessary laws and principles involved with the implementation of effective Marketplace Ministry.

Marketplace Ministry Action Steps

1. "Make your calling and election sure." (Read 2 Peter 1:10.)
• There are no part-time Christians. Acknowledge, then, that you are called to full-time ministry.
• Every one of us has a vocation—a calling. Redefine your vocation as your calling. Remember you are a representative of Christ wherever you are. Do not say, for example, "I am a salesman and I go to church." Instead, declare that you are "a salesman for the Kingdom of God, one who has a product or service to sell that gives me a marketplace platform or pulpit."

2. Define your "sphere of influence" and "your place of assignment." (Read Acts 16:16-34.)
• Wherever God has placed you is where you are to serve Him.
• Christ has a plan and purpose for you wherever you are and that is your "marketplace platform." Define your "9-5 window."
• Remember, you are *always* a Christian; therefore, you are *always* a witness in action and in words for Christ. Pray and ask Him to keep you alert and ready at all times.

3. Realize that the marketplace will be the proving ground for what you believe.
• There are seasons you will have to go through in order to prepare you for your marketplace.

• Each season has a timing, a purpose, and an active work to be completed. *In the present season of your life, God has you right where He wants you to be!*

• The season of work you are in right now should be filled with God's purpose! Read Ephesians 1:4-12. What season are you in right now? What further training do you need to move into the next season?

• Do you have a mentor and a spiritual father to whom you are accountable?

CHAPTER 2

Why the Marketplace?

I received a call one day from John, one of our church cell group leaders. John was a skilled leader, nurturer, and teacher in our congregation as well as a successful insurance executive. His insurance office was filled with agents who sought material wealth but also respected John's integrity and fair management style. He had even become a mentor and coach for many of the employees in his agency. The question he asked when he called surprised me.

John explained that Dean, one of the employees closest to him, had begun to ask him questions about his faith. But when John invited Dean to visit his cell group or come to church with him, his employee politely but adamantly resisted. Dean apparently wanted no part of "organized" religion. My surprise came when John asked me to meet with him and Dean for lunch. John felt that meeting me, the pastor, might pave the way for Dean to come to church or at least see that a pastor could be a real and genuine person.

I knew that the right place for Dean to experience faith in Christ and see Kingdom life in action would be at work, not in church. I also knew that the right person to lead Dean to Christ wasn't I; it was John. John had all the makings of a Marketplace Minister. He lived his faith every working day in his relationships with both his clients and his employees, and he did so right there in the marketplace. Dean didn't need to meet the pastor in order to see Jesus; he just needed to be around John. When John realized that getting people to come to church was not the answer and that the answer was within him, he was able to gain Dean's confidence, and so he introduced his co-worker to the One who had made the difference in his own life.

Why Is the Marketplace the Right Place?

"The marketplace is the most strategic and untapped segment of society for reaching and impacting the world. It is the place where the Christians and non-Christians live and work. That is where the lost, the confused, work and live.

"That is where the Holy Spirit is highlighting a place for the new move of God. That is the place that is all set for revival. We must learn how not to just take the wealth out of the world but to recycle it back into the world using their redeemed resources and talents in the most effective way." (Henry Blackaby)

Consider the following biblical facts about the marketplace in the New Testament:

• Jesus made 130 public appearances; 122 were in the marketplace.
• Of the fifty-two parables Jesus told, forty-five had a marketplace context.
• Jesus spent the major portion of His thirty-three years on earth as a carpenter before He began preaching.
• Jesus called all twelve of His disciples from the marketplace, not from the Temple or the synagogue.

God always prepares the person before He prepares the ministry. Jesus' ministry actually began at the young age of twelve. Recognized as an adult in the Hebrew culture, Jesus told His earthly parents that He "must be about my Father's business" (Luke 2:49, KJV). However, He did not engage in a preaching, teaching, and healing ministry until much later. The Bible tells us that Jesus returned to Nazareth and "was subject unto them," His earthly parents. "Jesus increased in wisdom and stature, and in favour with God and man" during the next eighteen years of His life. Then He began His public ministry, but it was not in the church or synagogue. It was in the marketplace. (See Luke 2:51-52; 3:23, KJV.)

Due to the acceleration of knowledge in the last ninety years, the marketplace has experienced more changes than in all the previous 1900 years combined. Most of these changes have actually occurred in the last fifteen years. Evidence of this was provided by *Business Week* magazine (November 1, 1999) in an article that was entitled, "Religion in the Workplace." This article reports that five years ago there was only one conference on spirituality presented in the marketplace, but today there are hundreds available.

Kingdom Passion and Impact

Yes, we have seen some progress in Marketplace Ministry. But much of the Church still seems to be operating within the old mode with old mind-sets. In Matthew 6:33, Jesus said, "Seek first the kingdom of God and His righteousness." So, what does this mean today, especially with regard to Marketplace Ministry? It speaks of radical commitment to and faith in Jesus Christ as one's Lord and Savior. But does that faith translate into a fiery passion to do the work of the Kingdom or do we remain only lukewarm?

Consider what the Lord said in Revelation 3:15-16:

> *"I know your works, that you are neither cold nor hot. I could wish you were cold or hot. So then, because you are lukewarm, and neither cold nor hot, I will vomit you out of My mouth." (NKJV)*

So What Does Christ Desire of Us? *Passion!*

A passion for the Kingdom of God must be birthed inside of us before Kingdom witness, Kingdom business, and Kingdom expansion will manifest through our words and actions.

> AN INWARD CHANGE THAT IS IGNITED BY PASSION, VISION, AND
> COMMITMENT WILL RESULT IN A PERSONAL CHANGE
> THAT WILL BE MANIFESTED AND DEMONSTRATED
> FROM THE INSIDE OUT.

> *Once, having been asked by the Pharisees when the kingdom of God would come, Jesus replied, "The kingdom of God does not come with your careful observation, nor will people say, 'Here it is,' or 'There it is,' **because the kingdom of God is within you**" (Luke 17:20-21, NIV, emphasis added).*

Jesus taught that the Kingdom of God is within us. He then described us as "the salt of the earth" and "the light of the world" (Matt. 5:13-14). Everything salt touches changes but nothing changes salt. We are to go out into the marketplace to change the world but not to be changed by it. Light dispels or displaces darkness. Every light makes a difference in the dark.

Our work, as a labor of love, should so penetrate and light up the world, that everyone around us is influenced and impacted by the Kingdom of God that is shining out from us.

As a Christian, I have believed my purpose in life was to lead people to a knowledge of the Lord Jesus Christ. As the sales manager of several large corporations, I was able to lead many people to accept Christ. I have had many more opportunities to do so on a one-to-one basis since I became a pastor. I now realize if we have a passion for doing whatever our God-given work is "as unto to the Lord," He will give us opportunities to change lives no matter where we are.

Of course, being born again is the first essential in this process. But remember, regeneration is the beginning, not the culmination of God's life-giving work of faith within us. From salvation on, our work's purpose must be to advance God's Kingdom. Our passion must be to fulfill our God-given commission. We must not allow ourselves ever to be lukewarm.

Passion in the Wrong Places

Read Matthew 19:16-22 which tells about Jesus being approached by a rich young ruler. Jesus looked with compassion on him, knowing that the young man loved God and was serving Him as a faithful Hebrew. Jesus answered his question by telling him, "Go, and sell all that you have and then give to the poor." This message was not about salvation, but rather it implies that the rich young ruler felt that he was righteous under the Old Covenant, but he knew he lacked the fulfillment of his destiny. Therefore, he didn't know what to do next. He believed his function had to do with keeping the commandments, which included going to the Temple. He had been faithful in doing this and in tithing as well. He did not realize he had a far greater destiny that involved using his talents rather than just his wealth. His wealth had blinded him from seeing the Kingdom that was waiting for his giving as well as for his ability to acquire and manage wealth. He did not know how to use what he had been given by God to fulfill his future potential. Jesus went on to explain to the disciples that if the young ruler could have detached himself from the control of wealth and followed Him, he would have accomplished more and accumulated more wealth, but it would have been for the Kingdom of God.

The rich young ruler who had great wealth "went away sad" after he heard what Jesus told him to do. The Amplified Translation adds that he was "grieved and in much distress." Why? Wealth can't buy salvation and wholeness. Jesus explained to His disciples that wealth provides no entry into the Kingdom, but it can be used to advance the Kingdom. (See Matt. 19:23-24.) The same gifts and talents that were given to the Lord for His use in Kingdom work are available to His Body as well, and these gifts are unlimited in their potential and productivity.

The people of God can use wealth to advance God's Kingdom here on earth. This is an important understanding for those who are seeking to have a vision and a passion for God's Kingdom to understand. God is preparing entrepreneurs who will rise up and shake the world by building and expanding His Kingdom. This Kingdom must be built on the Rock, the sure foundation. This Kingdom will then stand, not be swept away by the changing tides of circumstances or shifts in cultural sands. (See Luke 6:47-49.)

Once the people of God acquire this Kingdom mind-set, their actions and their words will be transformed even in the marketplace. For example, Zacchaeus was anointed to make money, but he didn't understand the purpose of money in God's Kingdom. Once he met with Jesus, his perspective changed. He realized he had a calling on his life to advance the Kingdom to the best of his ability by obtaining wealth. Jesus probably explained to him what His Father had said about wealth (see Deut. 8:18), and told him that it is to be used to establish covenant. Zacchaeus immediately began to give generously to advance the Kingdom of God by establishing covenant. (Luke 19:1-10). Zacchaeus was completely fulfilled when he fulfilled his purpose by using his money in the marketplace.

Zacchaeus's God-given sphere of influence directly involved money and finances. We may be assigned to that same area or to one of many other areas that are related to Kingdom business, such as administration, technology, management, human resources, or training, and the list goes on. The point to remember is that we are to be God's willing instruments. As we willingly accept our part in what God is doing, He will use us as kings in the Kingdom to transform the marketplace around us.

Kings and Priests Working Together

The Word reveals that God has made us to be a kingdom of kings and priests in order to build and advance His Kingdom. *"To Him who loved us and washed us from our sins in His own blood, and has made us kings and priests to His God and Father, to Him be glory and dominion forever and ever. Amen"* (Rev. 1:5-6).

God has called the *priests* to clarify and release His vision. He is also raising up *kings* who will provide the provision for the vision. The provision may not necessarily be money, however. Kingdom currency can include using and applying one's talents and gifts to advance God's work. Money usually follows as a by-product when God-driven people work with a Kingdom mind-set.

Consider the gift of administration with which God may have endowed you. Perhaps you are wondering how He is going to use this gift for His Kingdom. I can tell you that His Kingdom business greatly needs those who have the gift of administration. Whatever gift you have, God will use it as long as you allow Him to prepare you and position you where He says you are supposed to be. Remember, in Him we live, move, and have our being. (See Acts 17:28).

No part of your life is an accident. God has a perfect purpose and plan for you as you serve Him wherever He has placed you. As you continue to serve Him faithfully, He will clarify and expand His plan for you. You can only start where you are. You may not be called to serve in a position as a priest but that does not make you spiritually inferior. You may be called to be a king and serve Him in the marketplace. The Kingdom will advance to a higher level as soon as the kings and the priests have a Kingdom vision and begin working together in harmony.

Apostles Are Empowered to Envision Marketplace Ministry

And He Himself gave some to be apostles, some prophets, some evangelists, and some pastors and teachers, for the equipping of the saints for the work of ministry, for the edifying of the body of Christ, till we all come to the unity of the faith and of the knowledge of the Son of God, to a perfect man, to the measure of the stature of the fullness of Christ (Eph. 4:11-13).

This passage in Ephesians describes the different offices of Christ's ministry. The naming of these spiritual offices is not meant to segment the Body of Christ. Every believer can operate in each of these offices at any given time. This does, however, require us to be responsive to the Holy Spirit whenever and in whatever ways He wants to use us. We see an example of how Jesus functioned in all of these offices at the same time when He encountered the Samaritan woman at the well in John 4. However, there is usually a pre-dominant calling or gifting for each of us in one of these five positions.

Each of these five positions has a distinct job description. The evangelist is to win souls for the Kingdom; the pastors are assigned to raise and mature the saints.

The local churches, though, have put their pastors in a very difficult position. Their job description seems to include preaching and teaching, visiting hospitals and homes, ministering to the sick and the weary, and overseeing and administrating the functions of the staff and church.

It becomes clear that this is not His plan when we understand that God has put together a team to accomplish His Kingdom business. All of the Five-Fold Ministry Gifts need to be in operation in order to accomplish this mission. Therefore, along with the evangelists and pastors, God has highlighted teachers who will impart nuggets of truth layer upon layer, precept by precept. God's prophets are to point out the direction of the Lord to the Church. The apostles are to provide the vision and strategies to go and see beyond the church walls into the marketplace.

God has given a vision to apostles to go into the world—into the marketplace. They are called to understand and implement the very heart and moves of God for the particular time and season in which they minister. Jesus instructed us to occupy until He comes. (See Luke 19:13.) A literal application of "occupy" for today would be "to do business"—to do God's Kingdom business until He returns.

Now is the time for the Body of Christ to fulfill God's mandate and advance His Kingdom in the marketplace. We are to be one Body that is drawn together with the love of God; we're not to be independent but interdependent, if we are to accomplish the purpose of God for His Kingdom.

Religious Obstacles to Marketplace Ministry

In order for this to happen, old mind-sets have to change. We have previously discussed using our talents for building the Kingdom; let us now discuss some of the obstacles that might hinder us from doing so. We first need to examine the two most important commands that God has given us. These commandments represent the fundamental truths of God and the foundation of the believer's walk. We refer to these as the Great Commandment and the Great Commission.

There has been such an emphasis placed on looking for Jesus to return quickly that we have made the Great Commission seem more important than the Great Commandment. Both are of equal importance in the eyes of God and to His Kingdom business. However, He gave us the Great Commandment first.

Jesus said ..., "'You shall love the LORD your God with all your heart, with all your soul, and with all your mind.'

This is the first and great commandment. And the second is like it: 'You shall love your neighbor as yourself.' On these two commandments hang all the Law and the Prophets" (Matt, 22:37-40).

In Luke 10:25-37, we read about a lawyer who went to Jesus and asked some questions. He inquired, "Who is my neighbor?" and "What must I do to have eternal life?" He asked these questions because, in his religious mind-set, the message of Christ did not emphasize the Hebrew law. This created a longing in his spirit—a desire to settle his own soul while also discrediting Jesus in front of the religious crowd.

Jesus answered him by using a parable about life, the story of the Good Samaritan, in order to teach both this lawyer and the religious crowd. By depicting a priest, a Levite, and a Samaritan in this parable, Jesus eliminates all arguments about the Law and religion. He explained that the Law is not effective if it is not used in the marketplace. Instead, He gets right to the heart of the issue by using a marketplace businessperson in the story.

In this parable, both the Levite and the priest pass by a man who was half dead. They did nothing to fulfill God's commands that the lawyer had just quoted to Jesus in Luke 10:27. In other words, due to tradition neither the priests nor the Levites were able to *live out* loving God and loving others in a real-life situation. So if those from the priestly tradition couldn't translate loving God and others into real life when challenges and hardships came, then who could? Jesus answers this by using a Marketplace Minister, an unlikely king or business person, to demonstrate the kind of attitude that is needed for being salt and light to the world.

But a certain Samaritan, as he journeyed, came where he was. And when he saw him, he had compassion. So he went to him and bandaged his wounds, pouring on oil and wine; and he set him on his own animal, brought him to an inn, and took care of him. On the next day, when he departed, he took out two denarii, gave them to the innkeeper, and said to him, "Take care of him; and whatever more you spend, when I come again, I will repay you" (Luke 10:33-35).

Basis for the Marketplace

Jesus, of course, knew that the lawyer's question was a set up. Perhaps this is why He used a familiar marketplace setting to answer the question. The road to Jericho was a known trade route upon which business people frequently traveled; it was a place of commerce and daily activity. I am sure the lawyer had anticipated that Jesus would reference His remarks with regard to the Law and the Temple.

As we study this parable, we must first understand that the enemy desires to "steal, kill and destroy" the children of God, saved and unsaved alike. Like the man Jesus described in the parable, "this robber" will attack the person, and leave him/her to die and rot away on the roadside. This "thief" has the following attitude: "What is thine is mine. I will take what is yours even if I have to kill you to get it." He is hard-hearted and will deal ruthlessly with any unsuspecting child of God he finds on "the road to Jericho."

An extreme form of racial discrimination and hatred existed between the Hebrews and the Samaritans. The Pharisees considered the Samaritans to be "half-breeds," people who were racially inferior to them. Hebrews abhorred Samaritans so much that they thanked God on a daily basis that they were not like the "God-forsaken Samaritans," people they believed were of no use to God. Jesus was addressing this unhealthy spiritual atmosphere and dealing with it for all generations to come.

Jesus used a priest in His parable to represent the pulpit-type ministers, and He used the Levite to represent the workers or staff members of the congregations. Both had been blinded by legalism

31

and religious traditions, which had prevented them from sharing God's grace with those who were outside their "denomination" or doctrine. Since the victim on the road was naked, they could not tell if he were "one of them." They did not know his religious background or his station in life. Furthermore, according to their doctrinal beliefs, if he were dead, priests could not contaminate themselves by touching a dead body. This is somewhat similar to the exclusiveness that exists in some of our churches today. All too often people feel that if someone is not of their denomination or their socio-economic status, they are inferior to them. Individual churches can have this attitude as well.

Jesus is teaching us about the attitude of the religious priests and Levites. "What belongs to the church or God is mine. God has given it to me for me." Therefore, "What is *mine* is *mine*." God could not have expected them, a priest and a Levite, to give His grace to this half-dead traveler on the road to Jericho. What would be the point?

Both the priest and the Levite saw the man and deliberately passed by on the other side of the road. The Good Samaritan, though, had a completely different attitude towards the situation. His attitude was, "What's *mine* is *thine*." With such an attitude, this businessman practiced mercy and hospitality toward the dying man he found alongside the road.

The Good Samaritan shared what he had with the injured man even though he knew he would get nothing in return. I believe that the other two wanted something for their involvement and they saw no personal gain or benefit for themselves in helping another.

On top of this, it was an act of abomination for a priest or Levite to touch a dying man's body. Doing so would make them "unclean." Unlike the religious leaders, the Good Samaritan not only touched the dying man's body, but he personally cleansed and bound up the man's wounds. He even put him on his own donkey—his personal form of transportation.

The Samaritan then had the victim lodged in an inn for as long as it would take for him to recover. Obviously, this Samaritan was a person of sound resources and credit; he must have been a successful businessman. This example also indicates to me that fulfilling the law of being a good neighbor was probably a common practice for him. (See Lev. 19:18.)

He demonstrated the Levitical principle by not concerning himself with the cost of the treatment but by being motivated instead by love for his neighbor. He understood the principles of servanthood and stewardship. He knew that what God had given to him was to be shared with others. The motivation of the Good Samaritan was not that of the Law, or as we might say, "getting him saved." His motivation was to love him as he found him. The Good Samaritan demonstrated that practicing the Great Commandment leads to the Great Commission being fulfilled in our everyday lives.

The Good Samaritan Provides Us With a Marketplace Model

The Good Samaritan was a business person who used his time and resources to advance the Kingdom of God in his marketplace. He was a minister-on-call who did not find it necessary to leave his profession in order to join or start a ministry to fulfill that call. His business was his assignment to fulfill his call as a Minister for the Lord Jesus.

In other words, he realized that all believers are in full-time ministry. It was not necessary for him to leave his profession and start a halfway house or set up a "help the needy on the side of the road" ministry. Yes, the Good Samaritan was a dedicated businessman. Yet, out of compassion, he pleased the Lord by attending to the needs at hand and in doing so, he saved a life. He was motivated by love and believed God had set his agenda even in the marketplace.

In the Apostle Paul's first letter to the church at Corinth, he confirmed this truth by telling the Corinthians that each one should retain the place in life that the Lord assigned to him and to which God called him. He stated this as a rule in the church. He wrote, *"Let each one remain in the same calling in which he was called"* *(1 Cor. 7: 20)*.

The Good Samaritan did not care about the man's religious background or his religious affiliation. He was not concerned about the man's social status or family background. Neither was he concerned about the hospital bill or the transportation costs. He probably helped others on a frequent basis. He may have even had an arrangement with the innkeeper that made this kind of help a regular part of his ministry. It appears he was able to take care of his "ministry," then just continue on with his business with no interruption, thereby showing us that there was no dualism in his life.

The religious crowd, on the other hand, was focused on their religious rules and regulations. Their rituals had no value, however, because they were done without love. The end result was that they had ignored an opportunity to serve God.

I believe that this successful Samaritan businessman knew the Lord would provide what was needed. His focus was on saving a life, and he went to every length to do so. This parable provides us with an excellent marketplace model.

After sharing this parable, Jesus asked the lawyer:

> *"Which of these three do you think was a neighbor to the man who fell into the hands of robbers?" The expert in the law replied, "The one who had mercy on him." Jesus told him, "Go and do likewise" (Luke 10:36-37, NIV).*

The Church must understand that the world does not understand religion; it understands love and relationship. We are all called to be ambassadors of God's unconditional love to this world. So, if you claim to be one of God's ambassadors, then He expects you to express that love unconditionally to all who may cross your path.

Your "religious experience" may not be received by all, but know that even the most calloused skeptic can recognize love and compassion. Love is a universal language and currency in the marketplace of relationships. People don't care how much religious philosophy you know about love. They care about how much you care and how you show that love. This kind of love can and must be practiced in the marketplace. It is the foundational principle upon which the Seven Principles we cover in this book are based.

A New Season for Marketplace Ministry

All things belong to God, and, as believers, we are to be His workers for their distribution. God desires to bless all of His people so that they will in turn be a blessing to others, thereby proving to the world that He is God.

Jesus explained the purpose of His incarnation to His disciples and to us:

> I have glorified You [the Father] on the earth. I have finished the work which You have given Me to do (John 17:4).

> O righteous Father! The world has not known You, but I have known You; and these have known that You sent Me. And I have declared to them Your name, and will declare it, that the love with which You loved Me may be in them, and I in them (John 17:25).

In today's culture, we must confront the reality that the world sees little consistency or congruency between what Christians say they believe and how they really live. Some polls even tell us that there is little distinction or difference between a Christian's life-style and the life-style of someone in the world. Many believers have cast off absolute truth as being irrelevant and unnecessary as they live their everyday lives. As a result, relativism permeates both the Church and the life-styles of Christians in the marketplace. What is causing this?

When the Scriptures say we are to be "in the world but not of the world," there is often misunderstanding about what this means in everyday life, just as there was in the time of Jesus. The key to understanding this principle is found in the word "integrity."

The man Jesus demonstrated that righteousness and unconditional love are not contradictory; nor are they signs of weakness. Such integrity required that Jesus be secure in His relationship with the Father so that He could live in the world to please God, not man. Therefore, His significance didn't come from worldly acclaim, but from His relationship with God. He was living and involved in the world, but He did not adopt its life-style. Jesus demonstrated that man, with the counsel of the Holy Spirit, can be both righteous and full of love. He modeled for us how we can be strong, yet tender toward the needs of others. So we, as "man," can be godly and holy, and we can live a life that exemplifies integrity in the marketplace as well as in the Church.

In our world of consumerism, though, it is easy to be drawn toward the importance of economic power. It is vital, therefore, that those of us who are called to Marketplace Ministry understand that our security, our source, and our significance rest in God, not in a job or a position in the world. As such, we can move with spiritual authority in the marketplace realm, setting both finances and relationships in order. Then, like Jesus, we will exemplify that both righteousness and productivity are integral parts of the marketplace portion of our lives. We will then function in power and influence in the world without being influenced by the world system. And, as we do so, we will be working for God with integrity.

A New Ministry Mind-Set

In order to win the world to the Lord, the Church must have a new mind-set with regard to what winning and discipling the lost souls of the twenty-first century actually means. The message of the gospel, simply stated, is love. It is expressed through compassionate, unconditional labor. More simply stated, it is demonstrated through our service of love. It is easy to love those who love us in return. However, we are commanded to love all, even our enemies. We will see people saved in great numbers when the love of Christ motivates us and is demonstrated in *all* of our relationships.

Such love will attract the attention of the lost. All people hunger for affection and affirmation. When the lost are loved without any expectation of return, they will thirst and hunger for the motivating force behind such love. As we develop this type of relationship with them, they will seek to know the living God we serve. God's Spirit will guide us in loving them, no matter what their religious affiliation, their family background, or their social status may be. It is then that the Great Commission will be fulfilled.

I have discovered that highly driven business people often perceive Christians, who claim to love everyone, as being weak and ineffective in the business world. However, quite the opposite is true. Jesus was not weak or ineffective in the marketplace. As His disciples, we need to reflect His strength of character in the marketplace and wherever we find ourselves. I have made another important discovery, as well. Business people are desirous of knowing and working with people of integrity. To be known as a competent person of integrity, as the Good Samaritan was, is a witness that will win many people for the Kingdom of God.

Consider the disciple named Matthew. He developed a new mind-set about money when He met Jesus. As such, his renewed mind produced a life-style and ultimately a gospel that has won millions to Christ over the centuries. We need business people like Peter, Matthew,

Lydia, and Paul, people who can reach into the boardrooms and sales offices throughout the business world with the good news of the Father's love.

During Luther's reformation, we saw the emergence of the priesthood of the believer. In the present Apostolic Reformation, we are retracing the steps of the early apostles, and we are recognizing the ministry of the believer in the marketplace. Both of these emphases require faith.

This ministry of the believer in the marketplace is a new paradigm for the present-day church. It is a new wine that can only be contained in a new wineskin. For us to accept and walk in this present truth, we must allow our minds to be renewed by the Word of God, thereby removing all possible hindrances from our old, self-serving mind-sets. We cannot take this new wine and put it in an old wineskin.

We know that if we take a new cloth and sew it onto an old garment it will shrink and tear the old cloth. In a similar vein we need a totally new mind-set. We must first change our thinking, and then we must change our vocabulary. Our words must begin to reflect our new mind-set. We can no longer think or say, "I am not in full-time Christian work because I have a full-time job in the marketplace." Why? Because our new mind-set tells us that we all are in full-time Christian work. There can be no "part-timers" in God's Kingdom business. Therefore, we must learn and then implement the biblical principles of commerce, finance, and marketing. At the same time, we need to know how to relate to the people with whom we are called to work.

I urge you to instill this mind-set in you: we are *all* called to follow Jesus, to be His disciples *all* the time. This is our full-time vocation (calling) wherever we find ourselves—at home or at work. This is our calling when we're at a sports arena or other recreational facility. This is our calling when we're involved in politics or the local community fundraiser. Wherever we are, we are called to be Christ's ambassadors! Wherever we find ourselves is our mission field—the very place where we are called to serve and obey the Lord. Now is the time for the marketplace move of God. As we begin to do everything from this mind-set, fully aware that we are partners and co-laborers with the Lord, God will begin to open new avenues of opportunity for us, and He will bring success to our Marketplace Ministry.

Here is another old mind-set that must be dealt with. In the past, the Church has expected those who are paid by a ministry, usually the pastors, to do all the work of the ministry. Yes, pastors and teachers are called to train and equip saints, as we are told in Ephesians 4:11-12, but take a close look at what these verses are actually saying.

Pastors and teachers are supposed to prepare "... the saints for the work of ministry, for the edifying of the body of Christ." This tells us that the trained and equipped saints are to then go and do the work of ministry, which is edifying the Body of Christ, wherever God has placed them. Do these verses say "some of the saints" or "a select few of the saints" are called to the work of ministry? Of course not. Realize, also, that it's not just the evangelist's job to win souls. Evangelism truly begins with each saint loving lost souls in his/her own marketplace so others can be led to the Source of that love, God the Father.

As we renew our minds, we also need to put our priorities in order—we must love God first, then love others. Our first love goes to God our Father. As we develop our relationship with the Father, we can then love others. Before we can win them to the Lord, however, they must experience God's love in and through us; otherwise, our efforts might amount to nothing but dead works. The Church needs to train the saints with regard to this mind-set, thereby making it a reality in their everyday lives. Our compassionate actions will always speak louder than our religious words as we endeavor to evangelize others. We need to change our mind-set from the old evangelizing mentality to a new Kingdom focus. As we begin to work together in unity to edify the Body of Christ, we will accomplish much more than we ever did under the old "it's not my job" mind-set.

At the end of the story of the Good Samaritan Jesus instructs the lawyer, "Go and do likewise." Jesus answers the lawyer's original question, in essence, by telling him, "If you want to inherit eternal life, be like the Good Samaritan. Jesus commands the Church, His entire Body, to participate as Christians in their marketplace, to go there and lead others to Him.

When most believers hear this, they think it is all about winning souls. It may indeed be about winning souls, but it could just as easily mean restoring backsliders or helping others to prosper. "Go and do likewise" could also encompass assisting the needy, encouraging the downhearted, or offering help to anyone in need. The Holy Spirit may lead you to pray for the sick, bring a word of exhortation to the discouraged, or be God's hand reaching out to supply the needs of His people. This may mean mentoring another to his or her next level in God. We are called to go into *all* the world and become involved in the lives of *all* the people, even the disenfranchised. These people may need help with finding or improving a job situation. They may need proper or further education. Many will need economic-empowerment training to help them get back on their feet and become productive members of the Kingdom. All of these things are involved in the Kingdom mind-set.

Jesus used an extreme example to gain the religious lawyer's attention. Being a believer and having eternal life does not only address the question, "What must I do?" The more appropriate question these conditions address is: "How must I be?" You see, it's not the doing that counts; it's the *being*.

This will begin to become reality in our lives as we change our mind-sets and begin to create wealth by putting our resources to work for the Kingdom of God. We need to begin establishing an infrastructure and create wealth by acquiring properties, businesses, hospitals, orphanages, and many other such assets. It has been stated that 96 percent of the income of a church stays within its four walls. Many churches have "bought" the prosperity message, but they have failed to have a dynamic plan for impacting our world through Kingdom business.

Under the old mind-set, training with regard to the management of wealth and resources has been primarily focused on the individual believer. If economics are a part of God's Kingdom plan, then we need to bring our collective wealth and resources under Kingdom dominion. In the coming chapters, we will explore how to put all of our resources to work with a renewed mind-set and a focus on the expansion of God's Kingdom into the marketplace.

BEFORE WE CAN CHANGE OUR HABITS AND OUR BEHAVIORS, WE
MUST FIRST CHANGE OUR ATTITUDES.
BEFORE WE CAN CHANGE OUR ATTITUDES AND OUR MINDS,
WE MUST FIRST CHANGE OUR PERSPECTIVE.
SO LET'S BEGIN BY CHANGING OUR PERSPECTIVE.

Marketplace Ministry Action Steps

1.   Read Luke 17:20-21. In this passage Jesus tells us that inward change is ignited by passion, vision, and commitment, and this inward change results in personal change that is manifested and demonstrated from the inside out.

2.   So, what is your passion? Read Matthew 6:33.

3.   So, what is your vision? Read Matthew 5:13-14.

4.   So, what is your level of commitment? Read Matthew 19:16-22.

5.   What inward change is needed to exemplify "unconditional love" in your Marketplace Ministry?

CHAPTER 3

Principle 1:
Vision

PRINCIPLE NUMBER ONE:
GOD HAS A DREAM, A VISION, AND A MISSION FOR HIS CREATION.
WE ARE THE PURPOSE FOR HIS DREAM.
WE MUST UNDERSTAND THAT GOD HAS GIVEN US A VISION,
A MISSION, AND A PURPOSE THAT WILL FULFILL HIS DREAM
AND HIS MASTER PLAN.

Shocked and frightened! That's how I felt when God called us into the pulpit ministry. Mary was much more excited than me. We knew very little about starting a church! But the Lord spoke to my wife, and He confirmed that we were indeed to plant a church.

We had both been active as church members, and we had served in various positions within the local church. Mary had always been an outstanding teacher in both public and Christian schools. She had also built her college-age Bible class into one of the largest and most dynamic classes in the church. I had served in the office of an elder and as the finance chairman. I had also been in charge of raising the building funds for the church's facilities, including a school.

As a couple, we had been very active in helping an evangelist start his own church. I was earning a substantial income at the time, so just our tithe and giving were enough to financially support the beginning of this church. Mary provided help in teaching, and our home became the center of hospitality as this church was birthed. I was very much involved in business, and I was going through one of those business "harvest times." Any entrepreneur knows what I mean by that statement. The church we were helping grew quickly, and it continues to this day. We were blessed to be a part of it. However, we did not realize at the time that God was preparing us for doing the same thing later on in our walk with Him. By this time, though, I had discovered that God doesn't waste any experiences in our lives if we are willing to learn from them.

When the call came to start our own church, I was in the consulting business and had long-term contracts with five clients. These were companies that were preparing to go public when the window of opportunity for them to do so would open. So, as we obeyed and moved into this new venture with God, I was particularly glad for the opportunity to make the transition slowly. We started the church with nine families who joined with us. Obviously, our life-style had developed to a level at which it would have been difficult for us to stop receiving income. But I believe the question that was challenging me the most was, "Why me, Lord? I am a businessman, an entrepreneur; I am fifty years of age and I am seemingly at the height of my vocational ladder. I am enjoying what I am doing."

Although I loved the Lord and enjoyed working with the people in the church, I did not seem to have a pastor's heart. I felt much more comfortable with and really enjoyed business relationships. Actually, I had a passion and a heart for business and business people. Since God had called me to be a pastor, however, I prayed, "Please, Lord, give me a love for the people, especially those who don't seem to be able to *get it together*."

As time passed, I became involved with helping the emerging entrepreneurs and people in small businesses, the people God was sending to our church. My business background made their problems and needs obvious to me. Soon I was so busy helping people with their business problems that I wondered why God had called me to leave the consulting business in the first place. My expertise had earned me a great deal of money in the past and now I was giving it away. At first, I didn't understand this way of "doing business." I couldn't see what God was seeing. I didn't see the Kingdom vision.

As I continued to minister in this way, I began to discover that there were others within our association of churches with the same passion for helping businessmen and women in the marketplace. This passion for business never left us, but now it was being redeemed through a Kingdom focus.

Over the years we have been able to help thousands of business people become Kingdom builders, economic soldiers, and entrepreneurs for Christ. We have worked together to build a ministry that equips and trains Christian businessmen and women to restore the economic system to its rightful King, Jesus.

God took me out of the consulting business, and then He "recycled" me into Marketplace Ministry. His teaching and training revealed His heart for these "Good Samaritans" to me. I was able to refocus my gifts and use these same principles in His Kingdom work. I was now training and teaching those who were called to provide the economics and the enterprises needed to build wealth for the Kingdom. This wealth would now bring all things under His feet, thus accomplishing His purposes here on earth. This is the way it has been intended to work from the beginning.

By examining the lives of many biblical characters, we can see that God used them to bring about His purposes on the earth:

• Abraham and Isaac were anointed businessmen who spread their fortune among many. (See Gen. 12-24.)
• Joseph's life began with a prophecy and ended up with him being called to rule over an ungodly people and to protect and provide for God's people. (See Gen. 37 and 41.)

• Solomon was heavily involved in business, construction, and investing. (See 1 Kings.)

• Joseph, the carpenter, taught the young Jesus a vocation, setting an example of godly leadership and fathering that guided Jesus to focus on God's business. (See Luke 2:49.)

• Jesus chose a number of strong business and finance people, including a tax collector, as His disciples; these were Peter, Andrew, James, John, and Matthew. (See John 1; Mark 1; Luke 5.)

• Saul was a zealous religious business person before his Damascus Road experience. Jesus relates to Saul (who later became Paul) his calling, his destiny, and his purpose in one clear statement. God used Paul's business skills to greatly advance the Kingdom. (See Acts 26:15-18.)

• In Philippi, Paul met Lydia, a successful business woman who planted a church along with her business. (See Acts 16.)

Jesus told Saul that He was going to rescue him from his own people and send him to the Gentiles. (See Acts 9:15-16.) When Saul began his ministry, though, it was in Jerusalem a city that was very much like our American church today, basically without much of a world view. Because of this, God allowed persecution to come to the church. Many fled to Antioch. Saul went to Antioch and there, along with another successful businessman named Barnabas, was sent out by the Holy Spirit to other places to accomplish the work that God had called him to do. (See Acts 11:25-29; 13-17.) Saul, now called Paul, continued to go to the synagogues to teach the Jewish people, but he became discouraged and frustrated as the Jews openly opposed him and even became abusive towards him. (See Acts 18:5-6.)

It was at this time that the Holy Spirit sent two wonderful business people with the gift of exhortation and helps from Rome to Corinth. Paul had just left Athens and had arrived in Corinth where he met a Jew named Aquila and his wife, Priscilla. Encouraged by their example, Paul was "recycled" into business and began making tents with them. Because of this, they began to meet in homes, not in the Temple, as had been Paul's custom. Interestingly, this became the model that God, the Great Planner, used as He moved Paul throughout Asia and Europe to establish churches. God used all of Paul's skills.

If we were to examine the lives of others like David, Luke, Peter, and even Jesus, who was trained as a carpenter by His father, we would find that God brought them each through many experiences and varied vocations in order to fulfill His ultimate Kingdom purpose for their lives.

Everything I have been taught or have learned by experience is a composite of the ultimate work or vocation that God has called me to do. There is a desire within me to fulfill the dream, the vision He has given me to see the kingdom of economics and finance brought under the Church through the guidance of the Holy Spirit and the leadership of the Lord Jesus Christ.

I now more clearly understand the verse that Paul wrote to the church at Rome, "All things work together for good to those who love God, to those who are the *called* according to *His purpose*" (Rom. 8:28, italics mine).

God downloaded His vision into me. He does the same for each and every one of His children. Vision basically looks into the future to see beyond the natural, beyond the present, to see things as they could be. God's calling on your life is purposed through His vision for your future. God's vision for your future is revealed to you when you diligently seek Him. His vision and purpose are birthed within you out of His presence in your life. Once His vision and His purpose are within you, you begin to desire to see His vision and purpose fulfilled. God already has abundant plans available, which, if they are diligently and faithfully applied, will be profitable, prosperous, and productive in His Kingdom, and you will see His vision and purpose fulfilled. (See Prov. 21:5.) Through the following diagram let's explore how this all works.

God's:	vision/mission +	vocation/calling +	assignment/work	= Purpose
Vision:	What you do	How you do it	Where you do it	Why you do it.

Vocation and Vision

When God gives you a vision or a dream, your vocation (which literally means your *calling*) becomes very important in the fulfillment of that vision. You must understand that you are first a servant and a minister for the Lord Jesus. Your calling, therefore, is not your job. Your job is your place of assignment, and it becomes a means of delivering the message of your purpose into the marketplace. This means that whatever vocation God has you in, when He calls you and gives you His vision, will determine the direction of your ministry for the Lord Jesus Christ at that time. I am convinced by study and experience that if you are able to apply this truth to your work, you will be successful in the fulfillment of His vision.

This is closely related to the Principle of Workmanship and Stewardship, which we will discuss at greater length later:

> *Then God blessed them, and God said to them, "Be fruitful and multiply; fill the earth and subdue it; have dominion over the fish of the sea, over the birds of the air, and over every living thing that moves on the earth." (Gen. 1:28)*

God placed a "spiritual DNA" into all of us just as He did with Adam and Eve. We, too, were created with the purpose to be fruitful and to multiply. This is true in everything we do, including having natural and spiritual children, practicing good stewardship, investing our resources, as well as developing and releasing leaders.

Vision and purpose. The fulfillment of a vision begins with knowing your purpose and knowing why you are here on earth right now, right where you are. Knowing your purpose gives you an understanding of your role in God's eternal master plan. There is a purpose for everything and everyone,"a reason for their existence". The Scriptures reveal, "To everything there is a season, a time for every purpose under heaven" (Eccles. 3:1).

The key to purpose is that it is the linchpin or strategic connector that brings the individual purpose(s) to be bound or yoked to the Master Purpose of God.

Mission and calling. How you fulfill the vision is considered your mission. Your mission carries out or implements your calling. While all believers are called to follow Jesus, how each disciple lives out that calling will be unique to that person's personality, gifts, talents, and station in life. The place where you begin isn't your destination; it's just a platform from which you are launched.

Every mission is unique to the individual call of God on a person's life. Jesus had an earthly mission to destroy the works of the enemy and to set the captives free. (See Matt. 16:18.) It is that mission which led Him to the cross.

We have one purpose but can have many missions.

You have a mission which is shaped in the crucible of:
• seeking first His kingdom and His righteousness,
• loving God passionately and others sincerely,
• producing fruit that will last for His glory,
• developing your calling to a level of excellence,
• and learning to live and operate in faith.

Your mission has specific details that are unique to you and your call. God is the only One who has those specifics. So, as you seek His Kingdom and spend time in His presence, God will project, inspire, and empower your vision.

God will give you the provisions you need to embrace and implement your unique calling. You will come to understand His vision for you, recognize your calling, and discover how your specific mission for serving Him is to be completed. Remember, the resources and provisions you need to fulfill your purpose were created and put in place before you were even born. The key is learning to appropriate them.

The Essential Steps for Fulfilling Your Vision

How will your calling or vocation be shaped by the vision God gives to you? In your Marketplace Ministry, there are essential steps that can only be taken by you. No one else can fulfill your mission, your vision, your vocation, or your calling, though others will participate with you in the process. Having said that, let's discuss the first two essential steps that you must take:

1. Focus on Purpose – You are a "who." *A who does a what for a why.*

You not only have to have a vision or a God-given dream, but your purpose and the reason why you exist on earth at this time. In addition, you need to be focused on the mission, which is how the vision will be fulfilled. There are many Christians who do not know what they are called to do or why they are here. The result is confusion in their lives, which communicates inconsistency and insincerity to the world around them, the world to which they are called to be witnesses.

Christians who are clear about what the Lord is calling them to be and know the plans that can produce good fruit are fulfilled and full of passion. The results are consistency and sincerity in their lives, qualities which witness to the more abundant life that Jesus speaks of in John 10:10. Realize that each mission and calling is shaped by the Holy Spirit to bring glory to the Father. (See John 16:13-14.) We also know that God is a God of order, not disorder. (See 1 Cor.14:33.) As we learn to follow the Holy Spirit's direction, there will be fulfillment and fruit apparent in our lives, and these qualities will provide a strong witness to those who are around us. (See Gal. 5:22-25).

The Scriptures tell us that, as the Holy Spirit reveals specific details of God's plan to us, we are to write the vision down and make it plain so that others might understand and be motivated by it.

Then the LORD *answered me and said: "Write the vision and make it plain on tablets, that he may run who reads it. For the vision is yet for an appointed time; but at the end it will speak, and it will not lie. Though it tarries, wait for it; because it will surely come, it will not tarry."* (Hab. 2:2-3)

The more you make your vision clear, as you write it out and fill in the blanks, the easier it will be for you to find direction. If you have a vision that involves a business, a ministry, or your family, write it down and make it clear with evidence from your life experiences. Then everybody will see it for what it is and willingly join in to help fulfill it. This is why writing the vision down is so important. This is covered more fully later in the section where I discuss *planning*.

Knowing God's purpose communicates direction and inspires passion. The Hebrew word for purpose is *chephets*, which means pleasure and desire. God promises to give us the desires of our hearts. (See Ps. 37:4.) Since we have surrendered our hearts to Him, His Spirit now dwells in us. His Spirit will give birth to the desires and purposes of His heart within us as we read and study His Word. Purpose then fulfills His desire in His ways and in His timing for His glory.

GOD GIVES REVELATION BEFORE HE GIVES STRATEGY.

2. Develop a Structure (Organization)—This is to be built on principles from the Word of God, and it is to be established on a framework that is rooted in truth.

The mission and the plan to accomplish the vision must be structured so that others can join in to help fulfill God's purpose. For others to join in, the vision has to bearticulated and communicated and made clear. The mission to accomplish the vision has to be structured to the extent that others can relate to it and be inspired by it.

51

The vision of Christ for the Church did not stop at His death and resurrection; He imparted it to His disciples. The purpose and calling of the Church is to establish God's Kingdom on earth, and this was made clear to those Jesus left behind. The Kingdom of God becomes established as the Church when its many members join together and focus on the common vision of seeing the glory of God established in the earth.

Habakkuk 2:14 states: "For the earth will be filled with the knowledge of the glory of the LORD, as the waters cover the sea." Within His Church, there are local churches that are under the vision of each church's leadership. Remember, the purpose of the local church is to equip and train and empower the saints so that they can do the work of the ministry wherever they are. Some local churches will have a spiritual heart for teaching and equipping the saints for evangelism, to feed the hungry, and provide housing for the homeless. Others will be called to work with the local business people, while some are primarily involved in missions to the inner cities or overseas. There will be those that emphasize fellowship and family. However, all are instructed to pray, to praise, and to be salt and light to the world around them. This is what makes us one under the vision of God.

God's Vision

Here's the crux of the matter. You don't have the master vision; God does. God established a strategic plan from the very beginning that would accomplish His vision of a family in love with Him, a family who would work to establish His Kingdom family business on the earth. (See Rev. 11:15.)

God has purposed that we are to participate in fulfilling His vision and implementing His plan. We are blessed because we are a vital part of God's vision and plan. (See Eph 1:4-5.) We must know and understand that God is a visionary and a planner. He is not and never has been confused concerning the end result of His plan or how to accomplish it. He is not wondering whether His plan is going to work or not. His plan is dynamic, and it is based on man's response to Him. The plan of God for His Kingdom is guaranteed. His purpose will be accomplished. (See Prov. 19:21 and Isa. 55:11.)

God is the vision-holder and the mission-planner. Because He is a visionary, we who are born of Him have His "spiritual DNA" within us, and we are born to dream dreams and see visions. (See Joel 2:28.) Through His sovereign plan, God, the vision-holder, wants to deposit His vision into each and every one of us. God, the master-planner, has prepared abundant plans for us to enable us to accomplish His corporate mission.

> *"For I know the plans I have for you," says the LORD. "They are plans for good and not for disaster, to give you a future and a hope. In those days when you pray, I will listen. If you look for me in earnest, you will find me when you seek me." (Jer. 29:11-13, NLT)*

Our very life on earth is an integral part of His Kingdom vision. Our life mission centers on accomplishing that vision. We literally fulfill our destiny and advance the Kingdom of God as we work out that dream, that vision God has deposited within each one of us. Incidentally, the dream and the vision are not just about you.

No eternal destiny is fulfilled without a vision. Proverbs 29:18 clearly reveals that where there is no vision, the people perish. Every great accomplishment begins with a vision or a dream. Having God's vision is the beginning of success in our God-given mission.

Our future success is connected to the vision that God has given us. Because our heavenly Father has a vision and a plan which includes each of us, we must each begin to dream dreams and see visions. Our individual vocation or calling is our part of the overall vision that God has for His creation. Each of us was born in a certain part of the world at a certain time in order to fulfill our part of the vision, our destiny in God's Kingdom plan. God has a specific vision and a strategic plan to bring that destiny into reality. (See Acts 17:26.) No vision is accomplished without a plan—written or unwritten, spoken or unspoken. As God's Kingdom plan becomes a reality, abundant life will be fulfilled in each of His children.

You see, the core of God's dream, His vision for His Kingdom, is simply to have a family that will occupy His Kingdom. You and I are called to be part of His heavenly family. After the marriage of Jesus Christ to His Bride (the Church), after the Head is joined to the Body, the family of God will know and receive fully His vision. We are to be as one Body, and we are to live in love and harmony with one another. (See Eph. 4:15-16). Because God is love, the driving force for establishing God's Kingdom and accomplishing His plan is love. (See 1 John 3-4.)

Man's Vision

Man has a vision because God has given him one. But the vision will only become clear when man extends his faith and seeks God's vision. Revelation always precedes strategy. God gives the revelation of the vision first, and then He follows it up with how the vision will be fulfilled. To man's way of thinking, God often appears to give sparse details about His vision.

Although each God-given vision is designed to contribute to and be part of God's master plan, we each choose to be either a contribution or a contradiction to that plan. We may feel we are but a small, insignificant cog in God's great big eternal machine, but we are still an important component in His master machine. The choices we make do indeed make a difference. Remember, God is the vision-giver and the mission-planner.

In Acts 17:24-28, the Apostle Paul addresses an Athenian crowd about the unknown God. The apostle describes Him as the "God who made the world and everything in it" (Acts 17:24). Paul went on to explain, "He is the Lord of Heaven and earth, does not live in temples [buildings] made with hands [of man] nor is He is He worshiped [served] with men's hands, as though He needed anything, since He gives to all life, breath, and all things." Paul explains to these Athenians that this "unknown God," *"...has made from one blood every nation of men to dwell on all the face of the earth, and has determined their preappointed times and the boundaries of their dwellings, so that they should seek the Lord, in the hope that they might grope for Him, though He is not far from each one of us" (Acts 17:26-27).*

Creation Precedes Formation

You and I were in God's dream, a part of His vision, even before creation. He had us in mind as He created our environment. He knew us before we were conceived in our mother's womb. He confirmed this through His prophets Jeremiah and David in Jeremiah 1:5 and Psalm 139. God dispatched us into time and space on earth for a set time and a set place with a sure destiny to fulfill. As we come to realize His commitment from the smallest to the greatest details, we are amazed.

What a comfort it is to know that we are here because God has a purpose and a plan for our lives. Unfortunately, most non-believers as well as many believers don't realize their divine purpose for fulfilling God's vision. These people do not fulfill their divine calling because they do not understand the vision, purpose, and plan of God. Many are called but few respond; many do not know how special they are to Him. (See Matt. 22:1-14). This is the reason that many times God has to work through a small group or a remnant to accomplish His purpose.

The Church's Vision

God has been revealing His plan in His Word to the Church, the *ecclesia*, those who have been called out or set apart for His work. God began this process by establishing covenants and building relationships with individuals. This covenantal relationship between God and man, which is God's vision for His family, will be completed through the eternal Church, the universal Body of Christ, unto which all things have been given.

We see the consistency and patient persistence of God as we trace history from the first family of man and woman on earth. God had fellowship with them and He talked with them. Even though the first man and woman chose to break covenant with Him by allowing the sin of disobedience to come into their lives, God, in His faithfulness, still would not give up on humanity.

The Bible makes it clear that even when we are unfaithful, God will remain faithful, because He cannot violate himself. God is so focused and committed to His vision and His plan that He went to the extent of sending His Son, Jesus, the second Adam, to redeem all that the first Adam had lost. Jesus came to re-establish man's original relationship with God, tearing down the dividing wall between the two, by laying down His life for His family, His Body, His Church. Jesus Christ redeemed man's soul and reclaimed the lease of the earth. He put all things in place through restoration and possession.

The Church is God's great idea of a family. It is designed to bring us all together with all our uniqueness and all of our diversity to live in harmony as one family with Jesus as our Head. Our personal relationship with God, our heavenly Father, directly impacts our relationships within the Body of Christ. The Church's vision, as implemented through ministry, starts with a family relationship with God on a Father-to-child basis. To fulfill God's vision and accomplish His plan, we have to have an intimate relationship with our Father God, just as Jesus did.

Live Out the Vision

We have seen how God has a vision for all creation and for each one of us. That vision becomes our heart's desire as it is birthed within us by His indwelling Spirit. All humanity participates in His vision in one way or another. Those who refuse to heed His calling live empty, meaningless lives that are filled with insecurity, insignificance, and lack of purpose. Those who answer His call by faith discover an abundant life that is filled with vision, purpose, productivity, and success. As the Church trains and equips us to implement and integrate God's vision for relationship in our everyday lives—in our families, our homes, our personal marketplace and our church—we begin to fulfill His purpose for us. Of course, our family and church relationships are foundational and vital for us to be able to live out our individual callings. But we are not to sequester ourselves in our homes nor limit our relationships to just family and church members. We are to be in the world but not of it. We are in the world in order to change it.

Likewise, the church, in its local gatherings, cannot be a church within walls; it must become a church without walls. We are called to be salt and light, agents of change, in the marketplace. As believers who are firmly rooted in holy and healthy relationships in our natural and church families, we go forth into culture and society and saturate the dark places of the agora, the marketplace, with light. We become leaders and initiators of change, not imitators of the world's culture. We transform the marketplace into a platform to accomplish God's Kingdom business.

Now that we have an understanding of how God's vision for us will work within our lives, we can move to the specifics of how that vision progresses into the marketplace.

Marketplace Ministry Action Steps

1. Read Proverbs 21:5 and Matthew 6:33. Follow their instructions.
    • The crux of the matter is, you don't have a vision, _____ has the vision.
    • God's vision for your future is revealed to you when you _____. Out of His presence, His vision, and _____ are birthed within you.

2. Read Jeremiah 29:11-14. Explain what this means to your vocation.
    • God has already made available abundant _____ for you.
    • God's thoughts for you will give you a _____and a _____.
    • Revelation precedes _____ in God's Kingdom plan.
    • God is the vision-_____ and the mission-_____.

3. Describe your God-given vision. Has it changed since studying this chapter?

CHAPTER 4

Vision
in Action

M ary and I moved to Atlanta, Georgia, with our one-year-
old son, Paul. I began working as a salesman there. It was
not long before I learned that a good salesperson needed
to be motivated, have definite goals, and have an inward desire to
achieve. Although I had not yet learned about vision, purpose, and
calling, I did know I wanted to achieve, and I was driven to excel.

Two sources motivated me at that time. One was a book entitled,
Think and Grow Rich by Napoleon Hill. The focus of this book was:
whatever the mind can conceive and believe, it can achieve. This
became revelation knowledge for me, and it impacted me to such an
extent that I made specific, tangible goals, which I wrote down, put
in my wallet, and reviewed constantly. Incidentally, I was eventually
able to accomplish the goals this book motivated me to envision and
write down.

The other motivating instrument for me was a recording entitled,
"The Strangest Secret" by Earl Nightingale. Nightingale had set out
to discover why most people fail financially in the most affluent
civilization that has ever existed. After projecting the finances of 100
men, starting at the age of twenty-five, he found that only one of
them would be wealthy at the age of sixty-five. He studied the lives
of great men and discovered "the strangest secret." Though simple in
its statement, the deep truth he revealed deeply impacted me and
millions of others as well.

As a result of this man's research and revelation, Columbia Records sold over a million copies of his recording in the 1950's. From this beginning, Earl Nightingale went from "rags to riches" and became an icon of motivation. The secret he revealed became the foundation of the study and business of self-development. Nightingale's "strangest secret" was simply: "You become what you think about."

The Bible had revealed this truth more than a millennium before Nightingale discovered it. Proverbs 23:7 says, "For as he thinks in his heart, so is he." Later, Jesus reiterated this truth when He said, *"If you can believe, all things are possible to him who believes" (Mark 9:23).*

Earl Nightingale explained his "secret" by comparing the mind to a field. He said that a field is neutral in the sense that it doesn't control the kind of harvest one reaps from it. What you plant in a field is what you get as a harvest. If you plant the poisonous nightshade seed in that field, that's what will grow there. If you plant corn, the field will produce corn. In other words, you will reap what you sow.

In like manner, the "seeds" you plant in your mind will determine what kind of crop you will produce. What you think about will become your harvest. This is why it's vitally important for you to plant seeds from the Word of God within your heart and mind. (See Rom. 10:17.)

The Apostle Paul instructed the church at Philippi to think on positive things, not negative things. He also told them not to worry or to be anxious. It's so important to monitor what we think about at all times.

> *Do not be anxious about anything, but in everything, by prayer and petition, with thanksgiving, present your requests to God. And the peace of God, which transcends all understanding, will guard your hearts and your minds in Christ*

Jesus. Finally, brothers, whatever is true, whatever is noble, whatever is right, whatever is pure, whatever is lovely, whatever is admirable—if anything is excellent or praiseworthy—think [meditate] about such things. Whatever you have learned or received or heard from me, or seen in me—put it into practice. And the God of peace will be with you. (Phil 4:6-9, NIV)

My experience combined with the knowledge I have since gained, brings me to this conclusion. When God gives us a mission and a calling, we are to meditate and think upon it. What we think about, what we plant in our minds, becomes our vision. The more we think on it, the more likely we are to act on it and fulfill that vision. It's all part of God's wonderful plan. As we align ourselves with God's plan, then all things begin to work together for His purposes. (See Rom. 8:28.)

I have an expression I often use to remind people of this truth, "Dream your dreams, but live in reality until your dreams become your reality."

God's Progressive Plan

God created man in His image and likeness. He also gave man free choice to respond to Him or not. Since God chose to implement His plan through humanity (both men and women), there had to be many adjustments in response to man's choices. These adjustments would be based on man's level of faithfulness and obedience. God's plan is progressive, predestined, and sovereign. As we see the drama of events unfolding before us, we learn that there are great adventures ahead for us, including blessings, struggles, and challenges.

In the first two chapters of Genesis, God gave His creatures three commands that were and still are fundamental to the success of God's strategic plan:

1. Reproduce—both spiritually and naturally
2. Be fruitful—produce results
3. Take dominion—govern and manage God's creation.

We clearly see that God desired fellowship with the man and woman He created. He had given them instructions and guidance for a healthy, fruitful life in the beautiful Garden of Eden. It was God's plan for them to reproduce and expand the Garden to include all mankind. Even though they were living in such a paradise, they chose to disobey God's one command not to eat the fruit from the Tree of the Knowledge of Good and Evil.

With the Fall of Adam, God began to search for another man. In the twelfth chapter of Genesis, we see that He gave a vision to His faithful servant Abraham. The vision was limited in its details, but it was clear in saying that through Abraham's offspring God would establish the Hebrew children, the Israelites. These would be the ones to whom He would reveal His principles and His laws. From this one nation would come many other nations, and God's family would expand through them.

The purpose and plan of God remain the same for us today. We are all part of His great vision, which started in the Garden and was reinforced through the Hebrew children who were spoken of in Abraham's vision. God wants us to shine as light, to be an illuminating hope to a dark and depraved generation. We are to be salt, that which preserves the purposes of God, on the earth. As salt, we are agents of change who have been sent to prepare the world to receive the very nature of God.

• The Hebrew children were brought out of Egypt in order to re-establish the glory of the Lord on the earth and to reveal the one true God before other nations. God was looking for a people who would believe Him for who He is. They were to be available for Him to demonstrate His generosity and blessing through them, so all would see Him and know that He is God. In order to do this, God provided the necessary tools and gave Moses His instructions to be written down for future generations so that none should perish.

• Sometimes, out of ignorance, God's people have considered themselves as an "exclusive club," thereby eliminating others from the Kingdom of God. The tendency is to base our thinking on human judgments and limited human understanding. The Hebrew children, though, were to establish a priesthood of believers who knew that God wanted a covenant relationship with them. We have been instructed by Jesus to be one in covenant with each other, as the Father and the Son are in covenant with each other. (See John 17.)

• Through the Judges, God established the institution of government for His people. It was at this stage of history that God instituted some of the most fundamental principles for the nations of the earth. Many of these same principles are still in operation today.

• God used the prophets to point mankind in the direction of truly serving Him. The prophets were also sent to prepare His people for the coming Son of God who would eventually be the Head of the household of God's family on earth.

• Christ came, on behalf of the Father, to officially establish the Church on the earth. Jesus, being a full demonstration of the Father's love, brought full clarity to the plan of God to His people. Jesus represented true righteousness and unconditional love. He demonstrated to mankind that love conquers all.

The vision and calling of the Church now is to represent Jesus in this world just as Jesus came to represent the Father. We are to be a demonstration of the covenantal love of God the Father. We share the same inheritance and vision that God gave to Abraham, Isaac, Jacob, the Judges, the prophets, and the Hebrew children. Christ himself is the greater revelation of God's vision, and He has reinforced this vision for us.

The vision and heritage began with God establishing a covenant with man. The results will be that the kingdoms of this world will come under the Headship of His Son, Jesus, and they will function through His Church and become the Kingdom of God. Then His glory shall cover the earth as the waters cover the sea.

What is God's Kingdom Vision? (See Rev. 11:15.)

A Kingdom Vision is a heavenly vision. The vision of God is established. Our opportunity and responsibility is to bring that which is in heaven to be manifested on earth. Peter said, "Thy Kingdom come on earth as it is in heaven."

Knowing that God has given us a Kingdom vision, it is time for the Church to move from a "local church" mentality to a "Kingdom mentality." The local church will always have a significant contribution to make within the Kingdom vision through the equipping, training, and maturing of the saints, however.

Having a Kingdom vision with a Kingdom mentality means that we must first realize that we are called to impact the kingdom of darkness with righteousness so that it will be transformed into the Kingdom of Light. God's earthly creation is not a place to "escape from," but a place to bring influence and dominion "into." This Kingdom of Light is where the presence of the Triune God rules and the true King reigns. We are not called to live in or to be dominated by a kingdom of darkness.

When Jesus came to earth and defeated the devil, He established His Church and imparted His anointing to us, His Church. Jesus then sent the Spirit of Truth to empower and equip us, giving us everything we need to establish His presence in every area and kingdom on the earth. This includes all foundational components of society, including commerce, religion, government, education, and family. We are not to be in a hurry to leave this earth. We are to "occupy," as Jesus instructed us to do. The Kingdom vision is to bring all things under the dominion and Lordship of Jesus, the rightful Light-filled owner.

A Kingdom Encounter: "Nick at Night"

In John 3, Jesus had an encounter with a man named Nicodemus who had been closely observing His teaching and ministry. In spite of all the education and experience Nicodemus had received as a key religious leader, he realized that Jesus had something much more than he had ever experienced. Jesus seemed to have a different application of the Scriptures. Therefore, secretly, under the cover of night, Nicodemus came to Jesus.

Not fully understanding what he had observed in Jesus, Nicodemus said something like this: "I know the law of God and the traditions of men so well that I am considered to be an expert teacher of the Law, yet there is a depth, a meaning to life, and a power you have that I do not have." Nicodemus sought to know about this different and dynamic Kingdom that Jesus not only spoke about but had been demonstrating through His life and ministry.

This story reflects the same kind of emptiness that was exposed in the rich young ruler we mentioned earlier, the man who asked Jesus, "What must I do to inherit eternal life?" He, like Nicodemus, felt he had done everything the Law or religion required, but he knew that he still lacked the power. This is the same vacuum that is felt by many of God's people; they are yearning for "something more," for they know they are missing out on something. They probably thought they would find it through religion and may have discovered that religion brought them into a higher level, but they still found themselves yearning for vision, destiny, and a purpose.

Jesus replied to Nicodemus, "You have to be born again before you can see or enter into the Kingdom of God." There are two

65

requirements for entering into the vision of the Kingdom of God. First, there is a natural birth that brings you from eternity past to the natural world. Then you must have a spiritual rebirth; you must be born again, born from innocence to knowledge of the Source of life. Then you will be capable of seeing the Kingdom vision of God.

The Kingdom vision must be imparted on the inside before it can be seen on the outside. It is not something you do, but it is something you become from the inside out. Notice that Jesus' message was not "Come to My church," rather He was inviting Nicodemus to "come into the Kingdom." Jesus was explaining to Nicodemus that when you come into the Kingdom, you will begin to find your place in God's plan, and you will start to see God's vision and understand your part in His purpose.

Nicodemus, like most of God's people, still wondered how such a magnificent and awesome plan of God could be fulfilled from just a salvation experience. We have all at least thought, if we have not actually spoken it aloud: "Isn't there a more comprehensive plan for me; something more dynamic for my existence at this time?" What we need is to learn to view things from God's perspective and God's vision: When God sees some water, He does not see just a puddle; He sees an ocean. God does not see a single tree; He sees a forest. When He looks at you, He sees His vision, His plan, and His purpose for you. With His Kingdom mentality and perspective, you can begin to see beyond yourself and your own little kingdom.

When the rich, young ruler, who is described in Luke 18:18-23, approached Jesus, he saw only his own kingdom of righteousness and wealth. He had the local church requirements (temple law) in place. He had actually exceeded the expected requirements of the Law, but his priority in life had been misplaced. This young man's pursuit of wealth had kept him entangled in his own little secure kingdom. Jesus set before the rich young man a way to relieve himself of these entanglements. Although He loved God, his riches were holding him back from entering into the Kingdom. The young ruler did not understand the source or the purpose of his wealth. Wealth is a tool, not a pursuit. Riches are the means to an end, not the end itself.

To enter into the Kingdom is to gain God's perspective, not your own. Set aside what you want; desire what God wants. A Kingdom mind-set completely focuses on the King—His decrees, desires, and demands. With a Kingdom vision and a Kingdom mind-set, you become focused and have definite direction with regard to your destiny and calling.

Vision guides and draws you into your future. Vision gives you direction and enables you to focus forward. Keeping the Kingdom mind-set helps you to see the boundaries God has set for you. With God's vision before you, you can be and stay on course. Your Kingdom mind-set assures you that you have a purpose and that you are contributing, not contradicting God's plan. Vision energizes the people; without vision, the people lose courage and do as they wish, or they go their own way.

Jesus told Nicodemus that he must experience a spiritual birth to gain access to God's vision. Having God's vision enables a person to see what God sees and understand the heartbeat of God. Jesus had both of these capabilities, and He shared His resulting passion with the disciples, "The harvest truly is plentiful, but the laborers are few. Therefore pray the Lord of the harvest to send out laborers into His harvest" (Matt. 9:37-38). Jesus was telling them that their mind-set must extend beyond themselves. They needed to develop a Kingdom mind-set, see the field as God did, and become motivated to see the vision fulfilled.

We know we may be able to count the number of seeds in an orange, but can we count the potential number of oranges within those seeds? The disciples could only see from what they had been taught through tradition, but Jesus saw what God was seeing. A Samaritan woman first saw a Hebrew; then she saw a Savior. After the woman's conversion, Jesus said to His disciples, "I tell you, open your eyes and look at the fields! They are ripe for harvest." (John 4:35, NIV). Jesus saw a field of nations, a harvest that was ready to be restored back to their one true God, but the disciples saw a world filled with Gentiles heading for hell. While Jesus saw one family belonging to God, the disciples saw only forsaken outsiders who were considered enemies of God's chosen people. Jesus saw the dream of the Father; He saw the harvest of the nations on earth coming together to become one family; He saw God's Kingdom.

What do you see? Are you excited about what you see? Jesus was excited at what He saw. He saw God's purpose being fulfilled, and He saw His life in alignment with the vision of the Father. When your purpose and your vision are in alignment with the purpose and vision of the Father, you have no choice but to become motivated, inspired, and energized by what you see.

With Vision, It's Progress Above and Beyond All Lack

Vision provides you with a mind-set that will always move you beyond the boundaries of scarcity or constraint. When you have the vision of God, you will be motivated to operate beyond the world's law of scarcity. The law of scarcity simply says, "Get all you can, can all you get, and sit on the can." This is a mentality that says that there is not going to be enough to go around, so you must hold on tightly to what you possess. The Kingdom mentality, however, reminds you that whatever you tightly possess will possess you tightly.

In truth, there is no scarcity in the Kingdom of God. God's Kingdom operates in the principle of abundance and generosity—there's always more than enough. Therefore, your prosperity does not cause a lack in me. As a matter of fact, your success actually blesses and enlarges my life.

As we operate in the Kingdom mentality, we don't have to strive to hold on to what we have because we know God has more. In truth,

He wants us to give away what we have so He can bless us even more. Jesus told us to seek first His kingdom and His righteousness. Then God, our loving Father, can and will provide all that we need. (See Matt. 6:33.) The Kingdom is to provision what a financial mint is to wealth. Unfortunately, though, too many Kingdom people have a banker's mentality instead of a Kingdom mind-set. You see, a banker only has access to and is limited by what's actually in his bank. But the king owns the mint where the money is printed. He can make the money, so he has a limitless supply. Our King, the King of kings, has all the provision within His Kingdom "mint" that we will ever need.

When you establish the Kingdom as your priority, you will experience your personal wealth, business, and ministry going above and beyond your natural imagination. In His Kingdom there is an endless supply that will fulfill His plan and purpose. God's vision inspires and challenges us to go beyond good dreams to great dreams, to build the best teams and to achieve the greatest results, knowing He has all we will ever need to accomplish it.

When a Kingdom vision is combined with a Kingdom mind-set, a deep passion to achieve comes forth. This passion comes from within and is a result of what you are diligently seeking. Passion provides you with a greater capacity and a powerful thrust to accomplish the set task. Passion empowers you to do much more than you ever thought you could do. The vision will surely be accomplished as long as the vision-holder is willing to hold tightly to God's vision no matter what the circumstances around him might be. Life-changing, history-making events take place when somebody has received a vision from God and has passionately chosen to follow it through to completion.

The Effects of Kingdom Vision

With Kingdom vision, you can see what God sees. Your human sight and senses aren't enough to give you a God-perspective. God is saying to you, *"See, I am doing a new thing! Now it springs up; do you not perceive it?" (Isa. 43:19, NIV).*

69

Kingdom vision gives you God's perspective on all of life. It allows you to see a much broader view that goes beyond the immediate circumstances. Kingdom vision allows you to put things in context and not just focus on content. To look at the circumstances of life is to look only at the present situations or parts of your life. If you do so, you will feel that all things are not working together for your good. You will be concerned that all the enemy is throwing at you will overcome you. You may become afraid or discouraged. These things happen when your perspective is off and your vision is blurred by the circumstances in front of you.

Of course, we are not to ignore the daily content of our lives. But when our circumstances become our entire focus, the enemy will cause us to look more and more inward. It will be as if we are viewing life through a microscope. The Holy Spirit, however, empowers us to look more and more outward to get beyond the details and into the vision. When we focus either inward or outward, momentum will build in whichever direction we've chosen. To break a cycle or change direction, we must focus outward. Kingdom vision dictates what the details need to be; not the other way around. We need to make a quality decision to reposition ourselves to look from God's perspective and then operate in that context. At that point, we can then accomplish God's vision, no matter what the natural circumstances may appear to be.

Abraham was called by God to leave his family homeland. The divine instructions told him to simply proceed by faith to an unknown destination. Because Abraham obeyed God in this matter, God took him to a higher level and enlarged the vision.

He called Abraham out of his tent of small vision into the expansion of the universe and promised him that his descendants would be as many as the stars in the heavens. Again, God anchored Abraham to the context of his calling. What a vision!

God empowered Abraham to be able to see the following things:

- A baby would be born to him and Sarah even though she was barren and they both were in their nineties.
- Descendants as numerous as the grains of sand on the seashore and the stars in the sky.
  - A land of promise for him and his descendants.
  - A Seed who would bless the nations.
  - A city which would be invisible and eternal.

Consider the vision that God gave to Jesus. This vision came to Jesus as He neared the end of His earthly time. In John 17:4, Jesus prayed to His heavenly Father, "I have finished the work which You have given me to do." This work is clearly defined throughout John 17. Jesus had accomplished His purpose, which was to reveal to us the true heart of the Father. Jesus was a demonstration that righteousness and love could dwell together on the earth. The vision for Jesus to be the Restorer and the Source of spiritual life for all men was fulfilled through His intense unconditional love and His passion for us to know the Father.

In Luke 4:18, Jesus vividly declared that the Spirit of the Lord was upon Him and that His mission was to preach the good news and to set the captives free. When the vision appeared lost to the natural eye as He was dying on the Cross, Jesus knew that it had indeed been fully accomplished. He declared to all, "It is finished." His perspective gave Him the sight to enable Him to see beyond the cross to the Resurrection, to Pentecost, to the Second Coming, and to the eternal city of Jerusalem—to see a Kingdom without end!

Jesus came to destroy the works of the enemy and to restore mankind to God as His family, His Church. Between the beginning and the end of His mission, Jesus opened the eyes of the blind, fed the hungry, clothed the naked, healed the broken hearted, made the lame walk, and brought freedom to all who had lived in bondage. Jesus' mission, His reason for coming to the earth, was to restore the relationship between mankind and God that had existed in the Garden before the Fall. He was to bring mankind the revelation that we could again know God as our Father. After Jesus rejoined the Father, this restoration process became the mission of the Church, Christ's Body. Acts 3:21 tells us that Jesus will not come back until the restoration is completed.

If you see God as a damning, judgmental tyrant who wants to snuff you out, you will run from Him. However, when you come to know the true heart of the Father, as the Prodigal Son did, you willingly aim to become a part of His Church, the Body of Christ. Jesus came to show us a generous, loving, merciful, and gracious God. Indeed, He is so gracious that He is not satisfied with just being called God; He wants us to know Him as our Father. The Apostle Paul, understanding this, referred to God as "Abba Father" which simply means "Daddy."

Receive the Gift of Vision

There are thousands of examples of men and women who were able to see God's vision and then, in turn, to see how the vision or dream they had was a part of His dream. These people, though not recorded in the Bible, were used by God to change the course of history. I could use the lives of Martin Luther *or* Martin Luther King as great examples of this. The example I have chosen, however, is George Washington Carver.

There are many heroes of the faith in the marketplace. Many of these people received their vision from the Father as a result of the adverse circumstances of their lives. These folk want to provide a spiritual means for others so that others will be able to overcome "the curse." Therefore, these "heroes" become the ones that God uses to break a curse or a stronghold of the enemy.

Such a person was George Washington Carver. He was born to a slave woman who was working with a farmer in the nineteenth century. When Carver was a baby, he and his mother were abducted by raiders on horseback. He was recovered and brought back to the farmer, but not to his mother. The farmer and his wife became his foster parents. As a child, he became interested in nature, animals, insects, plants, and flowers. He had a beautiful garden that was adorned with different kinds of flowers from the woods, which he visited and nurtured early each day.

Although Carver desired to be literate and highly educated, there was no one to send him to school. Discrimination against the black race was extreme in those days, and the only school available to him was three miles from his home. At the age of ten he left his foster home to pursue his dream of an education. In order to do so, he worked for a family as a servant/cook. In this way he was able to obtain an education, and he excelled with his schoolwork. He was able to continue his education by working in a laundry job. In the process, however, his back became bent over as a result of too much strenuous work. Nonetheless, he continued this regimen until he was admitted into a polytechnic institute to study biology and natural history. He then became a member of the faculty of Iowa State College of Agriculture and Mechanical Arts and was in charge of the school bacterial laboratory.

George Washington Carver became a very successful biologist, horticulturist, and a great cook. He had a vast knowledge about plants and animals that amazed everyone. He became famous for his research with regard to uses for the peanut. The story is told that he asked God for the "secrets of the universe," and the Lord answered, "*Sit down, little man, and I will teach you the secrets of the peanut.*" His conscientious research enabled him to discover more than 325 uses for the peanut, 108 uses for the sweet potato, and seventy-five uses for the pecan.

At the time of his success there were many former slaves and sons of slaves who desperately needed help. Therefore, Carver helped to build a college, a polytechnic school, and an extension service for farmers that was free of charge. His fame spread so broadly that

Thomas Edison, another hero of the marketplace, invited him to join the Thomas Edison Laboratory and the Royal Academy of Science, but he declined these offers in order to help the local population and farmers in particular.

It has been said that Carver did more than any other person in agriculture and commerce to help in the elevation of African-Americans. He was given the Spingarn Medal by the NAACP, a medal that is given to the black person who has made the greatest contribution to the advancement of his race. George Washington Carver died of anemia at Tuskegee Institute on January 5, 1943, and he was buried on the campus beside his friend, Booker T. Washington.

You have a loving Father who has a Kingdom vision and a definite purpose for you. He is Father who is with you every step of the way. He has given you eyes to see what He is doing and power through His Spirit to join Him as He moves into the kingdom of this world and transforms it by His grace into His Kingdom of Light. God's vision of His Kingdom will be more than enough to supply all your needs, overcome your lack, and set you on a course to move into the world to live as Jesus did.

To be salt and light in the marketplace, you must embrace His vision. You are to advance His Kingdom into places that now know only darkness, pain, and death. You are to bring the living Christ into the home and the workplace so that the blind can see, the crippled can walk, the broken can be whole, and the captives can be set free.

God promises us that we will see visions. (See Joel 2:28 and Acts 2:17.) He wants to take any area of your life that is blind to His Kingdom and give you vision to see what He sees so that you can do what Jesus did. Are you ready to receive the gift of vision? If so, then you are ready to read on and discover how God will fulfill the vision He has given to you.

Marketplace Ministry Action Steps

1. Read Joel 2:28.
• Ask God to heal your spiritual blindness so you can see His vision from His perspective.

2. Read Acts 2:17.
• Why did Peter refer to this Old Testament prophesy right after the Day of Pentecost?
• What mind-set had changed Peter from denying Christ to becoming a powerful marketplace minister?

3. Read Habakkuk 2:2-3.
• What are you personally instructed to do?
• What promise is there for you to hold on to so you can stay focused with a Kingdom mind-set?

4. Write down what God has shown you and keep it always before you.

CHAPTER 5

Passionate Vision Requires an Army

here was a season in my life when I found myself traveling through one of those stretching, correcting times along my journey to significance. Ever been there? Four of us, all strong salespeople with strong entrepreneurial drives, had started an investment company by combining our clientele and talents. It had not taken long for us to grow into a large multi-million dollar company with offices in nine states, and we had diversified in many different investment fields. We were even featured as the *Entrepreneurial Company of the Year* in a regional magazine.

Then, through a series of circumstances, some of our own doing, we became too diversified and grew beyond our ability to manage our growing company. This caused us to go through some very adverse circumstances, including an investigation from the National Association of Security Dealers (NASD) and the Securities and Exchange Commission. During this very difficult time, it fell upon me to remain as the head of the firm. As the sales manager, it was felt that I was the closest person to the clients and could, therefore, better assure them that we would overcome these trials and tribulations without law suits and the loss of clients' monies while continuing to meet all of our financial commitments.

At this point in my life, my personal learning curve was heading straight up. I even felt that I had grown closer to God than I had ever been before. But while I was going through this trying time, I felt I had really let the Lord down. I pictured the Father saying to me, *"I gave you this opportunity and you blew it."* You see, I had always seen God as my loving Father as long as I didn't mess up. Incidentally, some years later, as I went through some personal counseling, I was able to see the root cause for this belief.

A Breakthrough Moment

Prior to these devastating circumstances, we had hired a hard-working salesman named Ray. As I spent time mentoring Ray, we developed a friendship and found we were both believers. When all this difficulty began with the company, Ray felt it would be best for his family and future if he were to join our previous sales manager, because he had been offered the opportunity to become a principal in that man's new company. Soon thereafter, Ray's beautiful young wife, Carol, was diagnosed with terminal cancer. We knew she was a strong Christian, but after hearing about her diagnosis, she had withdrawn and apparently did not want to receive any visitors. No one had seen her in several months, and the rumor was that she was dissipating and very depressed.

One Sunday afternoon we went to their home to give them a cake my wife had baked for them and to see how they were doing. After asking about his wife's condition, Ray asked if we would like to see her. In light of the reports we had received, I was anxious as to whether I could handle the situation, but nonetheless I answered that we would like to see her. Ray said, "Let me ask her if she would like to visit with you and Mary." Mary and I quickly prayed and asked God to prepare us to give Carol encouragement.

After what seemed like a long time, Ray invited us into their den where we made small talk as we anxiously waited to see his wife. Then Carol appeared. She was radiant and beautiful with the glow of Christ all over her. You see, she had been isolating herself with the Lord and had been totally absorbed in His Word and prayer. She had isolated herself to hear only from God and to avoid hearing any negative reports. When she appeared we were almost overcome by her radiant appearance.

The next hour was one of the most eventful, strategic times in my life. It started a series of events that led to the revelation of my true calling in life. Because of her circumstances, I was open to hearing the truth that I so desperately needed to hear. Carol was able to communicate to me that God loved me no matter what I had done, and that He had a great future planned for me.

She helped me to understand that what I was going through was not God punishing me; it was the work of the enemy. These were circumstances I could overcome through faith, just as she was overcoming hers. She gave me Scriptures to read as well as a powerful book on faith by Kenneth Copeland. God used Carol to give me a revelation that I had never known concerning God's vision for me. I received hope as I saw part of that vision. She was able to communicate to me that God did not have limits on me but wanted me to soar. I didn't know the details at the time but through circumstances, God would reveal more over time. In this way I was able to renew my mind.

Later, I called Kenneth Copeland, and he sent me all of his tapes. Not only did I do my spiritual homework early every morning, but I also listened to Kenneth Copeland's tapes on faith every evening. I studied, I listened, and I wrote down many notes in a daily journal. Here is one of the entries from my journal:

> God's unending, unfailing, and unconditional love fills me with passionate vision that cannot be quenched, sidetracked, or derailed. His passionate vision in me isn't just a solitary calling to be lived out in isolation. Rather, I need others to go forward with me.

This powerful truth has never left me. There have been many more times when I have missed the mark and probably disappointed the

Lord. But there has not been a time when I did not believe I had a calling on my life and a purpose to fulfill. It seems that most of us have to go through a breaking process in order to understand who we are and what a loving heavenly Father we have. It was at this time that I also came to realize more fully what a great gift God had given to me in my wife, Mary. After a time, Carol did go on to be with the Lord, and Ray has done extremely well as a financial advisor. We have remained good friends.

This experience provided me with a strong anchor for understanding God's vision for my life. His purpose for me does not change even when my circumstances change. God's love for me doesn't diminish when I fail to live up to His purpose for me. In fact, God's calling, vision, and purpose for my life depend totally on His love, not on my performance.

I'm not alone in my journey toward fulfilling His vision for me. God never leaves me nor forsakes me. My wife, my family, Life Center Church, and my friends in Christ support and encourage me, adding to me their measure of faith and encouraging me to go on and never give up. I'm not in this alone; in fact, it takes an army to fulfill God's vision.

It Takes an Army to Fulfill God's Vision

Carol also helped me to see that one of the great benefits of understanding the importance of vision and potential is the ability to see what God sees in others. Knowing this, I am now able to be an encouragement to others within as well as outside of the Life Center Church family. By seeing what God sees, it is easy to call forth and to prophesy to a person's inner potential and help them see it as a reality. Most people do not know how special they truly are to God. We are to exhort, comfort, and edify each other. Knowing a person's God-given dream makes it easier to do so.

In Ezekiel 37 we read about why the Lord took Ezekiel to the valley of dry bones:

> *The LORD took hold of me, and I was carried away by the Spirit of the LORD to a valley filled with bones. He led me around among the old, dry bones that covered the valley floor. They were scattered everywhere across the ground. Then he asked me, "Son of man, can these bones become living people again?"*
>
> *"O Sovereign LORD," I replied, "you alone know the answer to that."*
>
> *Then he said to me, "Speak to these bones and say, 'Dry bones, listen to the word of the LORD! This is what the Sovereign LORD says: Look! I am going to breathe into you and make you live again! I will put flesh and muscles on you and cover you with skin. I will put breath into you, and you will come to life. Then you will know that I am the LORD.'"*
>
> *So I spoke these words, just as he told me. Suddenly as I spoke, there was a rattling noise all across the valley. The bones of each body came together and attached themselves as they had been before. Then as I watched, muscles and flesh formed over the bones. Then skin formed to cover their bodies, but they still had no breath in them.*
>
> *Then he said to me, "Speak to the winds and say: 'This is what the Sovereign LORD says: Come, O breath, from the four winds! Breathe into these dead bodies so that they may live again.' "*
>
> *So I spoke as he commanded me, and the wind entered the bodies, and they began to breathe. They all came to life and stood up on their feet—**a great army of them**. (Ezek. 37:1-10, NLT, emphasis mine)*

God commanded Ezekiel to prophesy to the bones that they might live. Then the prophet was to prophesy to the wind, which represented the breath of life from God over the vision. These bones had to be put in the right skeletal framework and alignment to then become the mighty army of God's design.

You are designed to have life released into you as you align your vision with the design of God. This life-releasing power is the anointing of God that destroys yokes and removes burdens. But it is not God's plan for you to be a one-man army. There are many diverse talents, weapons, and tools that are to work together to form this powerful army.

History shows us that it takes more than one person to fulfill a vision. Leviticus 26:8 makes this clear: "Five of you shall chase a hundred, and a hundred of you shall put ten thousand to flight; your enemies shall fall by the sword before you." We call this team synergy. God is a team—the Father, the Son, and the Holy Spirit. Everything they do they do together. Remember this acronym: TEAM—Together Everyone Accomplishes Much!

God will have others who share in or relate to your God-given vision team up with you in various capacities to fulfill that vision. Let me share with you an example of one man in history who pulled together an army to implement God's Kingdom vision.

Martin Luther King, Jr.—A Passionate Visionary Who Mobilized an Army

The Rev. Dr. Martin Luther King, Jr. was a superb communicator. He was able to bring clarity and passion to his God-given vision. Thousands who shared his dream were drawn to him as he powerfully articulated his vision and mission through his speeches and his life. We can experience the power of vision as we revisit a small segment of his famous historical speech that was given in Washington, D.C., on August 28, 1963:

"When the architects of our republic wrote the magnificent words of the Constitution and the Declaration of Independence, they were signing a promissory note to which every American was to fall heir. This note was a promise that all men, yes, black men as well as white men, would be guaranteed the 'unalienable Rights' of 'Life, Liberty and the pursuit of Happiness'."

Dr. King made it clear to all who were listening in front of the Lincoln Memorial and on radio and television on that historic day that in the light of God's plan of reconciliation, all men should be considered equal.

Measuring society's performance against the vision of God, he said, "It is obvious today that America has defaulted on this promissory note, insofar as her citizens of color are concerned." He went on to declare, "And so, we've come to cash this check — a check that will give us upon demand the riches of freedom and the security of justice." Martin Luther King's vision was obviously deeply rooted in God's vision for all people.

Then Dr. King explained his dream:

"I say to you today, my friends, so even though we face the difficulties of today and tomorrow, I still have a dream. It is a dream deeply rooted in the American dream. I have a dream that one day this nation will rise up and live out the true meaning of its creed: 'We hold these truths to be self-evident, that all men are created equal.' I have a dream that one day on the red hills of Georgia, the sons of former slaves and the sons of former slave owners will be able to sit down together at the table of brotherhood. I have a dream that one day even the state of Mississippi, a state sweltering with the heat of injustice, sweltering with the heat of oppression, will be transformed into an oasis of freedom and justice."

What Martin Luther King, Jr. saw in his dream was God's vision for the Church. The Church is comprised of people from different social, economic, and ethnic backgrounds, people of all races and colors, all becoming God's family—all one in Him. Dr. King substantiates his speech by quoting Isaiah 40:5: "And the glory of the Lord shall be revealed, and all flesh shall see it together."

He ended his speech with these words:

"And when this happens, when we allow freedom to ring, when we let it ring from every village and every hamlet, from every state and every city, we will be able to speed up that day when *all* of God's children, black men and white men, Jews and Gentiles, Protestants and Catholics, will be able to join hands and sing in the words of the old Negro spiritual: *'Free at last! Free at last! Thank God Almighty, we are free at last!'*"

Dr. King's dream was the vision that God had put in his spirit as a purpose that had to be fulfilled. Martin Luther King, Jr. then embarked on a mission that led him to become a powerful civil rights leader. When we hear about a dream that comes from a passionate soul, we are inspired. Dr. King's speech, delivered to more than 250,000 from the steps of the Lincoln Memorial, came from a passion that was deep inside. As a matter of fact, the last part of his speech came directly from his heart, not from any written notes. This passion came from going to the mountaintop and seeing what God was seeing: *Freedom and Truth.*

Passionate Vision Needs Structure and a Team

The passion that is within has to have a structure in order for it to produce results. It must be encompassed in a mission with a purpose so that others of like passion can join in and work together to fulfill the vision. This is the same pattern Jesus used to impart vision to His disciples. His was a passion so powerful that it would not let them stop until His vision was fulfilled.

To accomplish the passionate vision Martin Luther King spoke of in his historic speech, a structure and an organization needed to be established behind it. The result was the formation of the Southern Christian Leadership Council. Those who identified with his vision and were willing to work to see it accomplished were invited to join with Dr. King. Within this organized structure there were those who would carry the banner or go to Alabama to engage in a protest. Just as important, though, were those who were called to help by sending out letters or doing administrative work. Through the creation of a business organization, a legal entity is established, and this makes it possible for the group to gain access to resources and to function on a much higher level than one person could do alone.

This same principle is true at The Life Center where I am the Senior Pastor and Apostle. We had to develop an organized structure in order to propagate the vision God gave to us—the vision to train, equip, empower, and activate others to go forth and impact their world. The visions God gives to His Church do not conflict with His Kingdom agenda. They will certainly not contradict any of God's basic principles of stewardship, workmanship, values, and integrity.

The Passion of Jesus to Build His Army, the Church

Remember, God's vision for His Church, the reason He sent Jesus to earth, was that His Body would become the greatest force on the earth. This brings us to the issues of vision and vocation.

Jesus' passion was and is for all people to know the Father as He knows Him. This is the light or revelation He brought to earth. This is the same light that we bring to darkness and ignorance. Jesus and the Father have a vision of seeing a unified and united family. Jesus' purpose was to show us the Father's heart. His mission was to bring heaven to earth, to restore the rightful position and power of believers as part of the Father's family. All too often, however, religion has replaced relationship in local churches.

In the fourth chapter of John, we see Jesus, the man, when He was physically tired from His journey through Samaria. He stopped to rest at a well while His disciples went to buy food. There, at the well, Jesus had an encounter with a Samaritan woman. Through His prophetic dialogue, while working through the religious talk, He revealed to her who He was and still is today. She was immediately overjoyed and set free. Then she left her water jars and was activated. She even started a church. When the disciples returned, they found Jesus energized to such an extent that they thought He had eaten. His energy had come from being "on purpose," from remaining focused on what He was called to do.

Jesus was fulfilling His purpose and mission. He had been able to reveal His purpose—to show the Father's heart to this outcast, ostracized, "half-breed," and to see her come into the Father's family. He saw His mission of coming to establish the Church being fulfilled. This purpose, this vision of a body of believers from all cultures and all ethnic groups, was being realized. His passion came from His purpose. "My food," said Jesus, "is to do the will of him who sent me and to finish His work." Jesus then spoke of His vision to the disciples:

> *Do you not say, 'Four months more and then the harvest'? I tell you, open your eyes and look at the fields! They are ripe for harvest. Even now the reaper draws his wages, even now he harvests the crop for eternal life, so that the sower and the reaper may be glad together. (John 4:34-36, NIV)*

Jesus' disciples did not see the vision of the Church because they were still expecting Jesus to establish a Jewish kingdom. They did not see the Samaritans as a part of the Church, the organization, the army Jesus was building to carry on God's plan.

Jesus went on to emphasize to the disciples that this was not an isolated venture, but the result of a team or an army working together. He said, *"Thus the saying 'One sows and another reaps' is true. I sent you to reap what you have not worked for. Others have done the hard work, and you have reaped the benefits of their labor" (John 4:37-38, NIV).*

God's principles are His thoughts and they give the boundaries for mankind, allowing the vision to go forth. You will be successful in your mission if you follow His principles, thereby guiding your life by His thoughts and remaining within His given boundaries.

Add passion to this equation and you have the life that vision needs to even put flesh on dry bones. As others come alive in Christ, they can be motivated by your passionate vision to join in with you. Then they can be mobilized into an army to move forward with you as a team that fulfills the plans and purposes of God for His Kingdom.

The vision that God has given to you for marketplace ministry needs an army—a team that is motivated by passion. This team will work together to effectively advance God's Kingdom. Without vision, the team perishes and dreams dissipate. However, with a passionate vision before them, an organized team becomes a corporate body working together and moving forward into God's future. How does this happen? Once a team is in place, what specifics must be implemented? This will be the next topic for our consideration.

Marketplace Ministry Action Steps

1. Did you ever feel as if God was punishing you for not living up to His expectations? Describe that experience.

2. What did you learn from this chapter that changes your mind-set concerning trials and tribulations in your life?

3. Complete this powerful statement: God's calling, vision, and purpose for your life depend totally on His _____, not on your_____.

4.   "The vision that God has given you for marketplace ministry needs an army, a team that is motivated by passion—a team that will work together to effectively advance His Kingdom."

• Based on this, begin thinking of those who may share your vision.

• Ask the Lord to reveal to you those who are of a like mind with you.

• Begin to pray for your team.

5.   Write down whatever the Holy Spirit reveals to you during this preparation time.

6.   Also pray for God to begin to share with you His plans for the structure you will need to organize your team.

7.   Again, write down everything He shows you, even if it does not make sense to you right now. Remember, His thoughts are higher than yours.

CHAPTER 6

The Specifics of Vision

W hen God initially reveals a vision to you, it may not be what you think it is going to be and it may not happen when you think it is going to happen. Everything good happens in God's own timing; we have to be patient and persistent. A vision can be taken further and to greater heights in God as you team up with and honor the vision holder.

When God gave the vision of The Life Center, it came as a literal vision that He gave first to my wife. At the time I did not even believe women should be in ministry. So I had to work and pray through all these preconceived notions in order to align myself with the vision and to honor my wife as the founding pastor.

To complicate matters, my wife was a prophet, and I did not understand the prophetic realm. My wife also believed in deliverance, and that was not part of my theology either. I felt intimidated by those I had observed in deliverance ministry. So I prayed and asked God to leave deliverance out of our ministry. Thank God for His grace and mercy which were at work within me through those years. His grace and mercy continue to keep me from missing God's full vision.

Vision Always Stretches You and Takes You to a Higher Level

Many of us are not able to receive the full revelation of a God-given vision right away. This could be as a result of our life experiences, a need to change attitudes, or simply coming to the end of ourselves by putting personal agendas aside. Once distractions are removed, we are able to see what God sees. God's vision looks beyond just the vision holder.

Because time and space do not limit God, the vision He gives to you may be greater than you can fully accomplish in your lifetime. The higher you go in God, the more you will seek Him, and He will impart even greater visions to you.

For example, Peter's vision was hindered until he fully realized who Jesus was and the full extent of His mission on earth. Jesus had to rebuke him because he did not see the vision of God: *"Get behind me, Satan! You are a stumbling block to me; you do not have in mind the things of God, but the things of men" (Matt. 16:23, NIV)*. Once Peter had set aside his own agendas and beliefs, he could truly become "the rock." (See Matt 16:18.)

In order for Christ's vision within us to live, we have to die to self. (See Gal. 2:20-21.) We might even be called to die to the vision itself in order for resurrection power to truly bring it to life. Consider the vision God gave to Abraham; it was a vision of his descendents inheriting the earth. Abraham and Sarah believed in the vision but conspired to create their own agenda and birth that vision in their own way.

Using the maidservant Hagar, Abraham and Sarah birthed Ishmael, who represented man's vision, not God's. Perhaps it was a good idea, but it was not a God idea. It was a short-term solution which could never meet God's long-term goal. When Abraham and Sarah finally obeyed God, they birthed His vision, Isaac. When God's vision moves in, your vision must move out. That's why Ishmael along with Hagar had to leave.

God stretched Abraham and Sarah even further when He asked them to put Isaac on the altar atop Mount Moriah. Your journey up toward God's vision may lead you to an altar instead of a summit in your life. There Abraham was willing to kill the vision, die to the dream, and surrender all to God. In that moment of complete obedience and surrender, God resurrected the vision. Isaac lived. Abraham learned that *Yahweh Jireh* was his provision. He learned that his provision did not come from the vision, his own wit, or any other resources. God's vision had "stretched him" and taken him to a higher level.

Vision Takes Us Beyond Personal Salvation

I first learned about vision not in a church but in a corporate setting. I enjoyed corporate strategic planning because I could clearly see the benefits of setting up an organization. Realizing later that God is also a strategic planner, I began to see that His plan was far greater than the salvation experience alone. It included the redemption of all creation. Jesus said that He came "to save *that* which was lost," not just *those* who were lost. (See Luke 15:4.) His mission extends into all areas of creation, and, on a personal level, it begins with our personal salvation.

Paul writes:

For the earnest expectation of the creation eagerly waits for the revealing of the sons of God. For the creation was subjected to futility, not willingly, but because of Him who subjected it in hope; because the creation itself also will be delivered from the bondage of corruption into the glorious liberty of the children of God. For we know that the whole creation groans and labors with birth pangs together until now. Not only that, but we also who have the firstfruits of the Spirit, even we ourselves groan within ourselves, eagerly waiting for the adoption, the redemption of our body. (Rom. 8:19-23, NKJV)

Jesus reconciled us to God, and His reconciliation includes the whole world:

> *Now all things are of God, who has reconciled us to Himself through Jesus Christ, and has given us the ministry of reconciliation, that is, that God was in Christ reconciling the world to Himself, not imputing their trespasses to them, and has committed to us the word of reconciliation. (2 Cor. 5:18-19, NKJV)*

I began to see that God has not forsaken the original vision He gave to man in those first chapters of Genesis. We are still to be fruitful and multiply. We are still to take dominion over the earth and subdue it. I now realize, though, that to fulfill such a mandate will require time and a great many people.

Vision Must Be Transgenerational

Fulfilling God's vision could even require more than one generation. This may even be true of a particular portion of the overall vision. A vision may span more than one generation of vision holders who beautifully blend together to complete the picture. The Bible often refers to Abraham, Isaac, and Jacob and exemplifies how Isaac and then Jacob carried the vision that had been given to Abraham; they kept it going from generation to generation.

The vision you now hold may be an extension of a vision that was begun generations before you. After the initial vision holder passes, the vision does not die. Instead, the next generation picks it up and carries it on to the next level. The greater the vision and the higher the calling, the more important it is for transgenerational succession to be carefully planned.

All through history, we see how particular God was in choosing the "vision successors." Remember, *God has to prepare us for what*

He has prepared for us. Like Abraham, we are not to be intimidated by the vision. Rather, we need to allow God to perform miracles in our lives. As we obey and surrender in the same way Abraham did, God will demonstrate His generosity and provision.

Consider the consequences that result from limiting God's dream for you. In 2 Kings 13:15-19, the dying Elisha gave some specific instructions to Jehoash, the King of Israel:

> *And Elisha said to him, "Take a bow and some arrows."*
> *So he took himself a bow and some arrows. Then he said to*
> *the king of Israel, "Put your hand on the bow." So he put his*
> *hand on it, and Elisha put his hands on the king's hands. And*
> *he said, "Open the east window"; and he opened it. Then Elisha*
> *said, "Shoot"; and he shot. And he said, "The arrow of the*
> *LORD's deliverance and the arrow of deliverance from Syria;*
> *for you must strike the Syrians at Aphek till you have destroyed*
> *them." Then he said, "Take the arrows;" so he took them. And*
> *he said to the king of Israel, "Strike the ground"; so he struck*
> *three times, and stopped. And the man of God was angry with*
> *him, and said, "You should have struck five or six times; then*
> *you would have struck Syria till you had destroyed it! But*
> *now you will strike Syria only three times."*

The king obeyed Elisha's instructions to a certain extent, but because his vision was too small and his passion was too lukewarm, he placed limitations on what had been purposed for him.

God will test you before He will take you to the next level of His vision. The test for Abraham was to see if Isaac was more important to him than his obedience to and his relationship with God. If it had been, then Isaac would have become his god. Your vision must never become your idol or your god! Only God is the vision-giver. Only God has the specifics with regard to how His vision is to be fulfilled.

The Specifics or Objectives of the Vision

God gives us the vision and then the strategies to move that vision forward. When we receive a vision and the specifics concerning how we are to accomplish it, we are then to fulfill the mission. Every mission must have set objectives. Objectives are specific goals or benchmarks that must be accomplished to move the mission forward. These are the key elements that are to be completed within specific time frames in order to accomplish the overall mission.

We have previously discussed Jesus' purpose for coming to earth, which was to show heart of the Father to mankind. Jesus knew He had specific steps or objectives to accomplish in order to fulfill His mission and vision. Jesus knew that by accomplishing these objectives, He could remove the restrictions of sin that came through the Fall. In this way He would be able to restore man's intimacy with God, the Father. Setting us free from sin and death included defeating the works of the enemy and performing miracles to demonstrate the heart and power of the Father.

In Hebrews 12:1-2, we see that Jesus did not let anything distract Him from accomplishing those objectives:

> *Therefore we also, since we are surrounded by so great a cloud of witnesses, let us lay aside every weight, and the sin which so easily ensnares us, and let us run with endurance the race that is set before us, looking unto Jesus, the author and finisher of our faith, who for the joy that was set before Him endured the cross, despising the shame, and has sat down at the right hand of the throne of God.*

Write the Vision

The objectives in your plan or vision are the girders of steel in the bridge that spans the gap between where you are to the other side of your goal. When the Lord begins to give you revelations concerning the vision, you must be faithful to write them down.

There are many people in the Body of Christ who have no idea of the magnificent vision of God and the tactical part they are to play within it. Writing down your objectives helps to give you focus, and it communicates the vision God has set before you to others. In this way you can begin to build the team you'll need to accomplish those objectives.

Align and Merge Your Vision With the Vision of Others

Once you know your objectives, you need to align your vision with that of other vision builders. Abraham was the only one who heard the voice of God, but he related what he heard to those who followed. This is why a planned succession is so important. People may see the vision and have a common vision with you, but they may do so with a different purpose and mission in mind. Those with individual visions can work together for the common vision so that the Kingdom of God will continue to advance. The Apostle Paul compared this principle with the smooth functioning of a body, even though a body is comprised of different gifts and talents. (See Rom. 12:4-5 and 1 Cor. 12:12.)

For a merging of visions to occur, though, there must be a platform for this coming together. That platform is the Church, which holds the corporate vision for His Body to be a force in the world. A primary venue for implementing this corporate vision is marketplace ministry. The Church is not to retreat behind cloistered walls to worship and work. Rather, we are to form a mighty army that steadily advances into the world, transforming the worldly kingdoms into His Kingdom of Light.

God lays out a vision through a person He trusts. God sends that individual forth as a pioneer who carries the vision and forges out missions that literally change the world. As one vision merges and works with another vision, they achieve an even greater purpose. Merging of visions occurs when you have one or more vision holders teaming up with each another to accomplish a larger common vision. Those who are drawn to join together must honor the larger, common vision or there will be division. The Apostle James calls this a "double vision." (See James 1:8.) There can be merging of visions, but there must not be division.

In the corporate world, the success of a merger or an acquisition depends on the participating companies' ability to merge their visions and values into one new corporate vision. To determine the possibility of success, they must first evaluate whether they have similar or incompatible cultures. The corporate culture stems from establishing the core values that came from the original vision holder. The vision and values of each organization must be carefully examined to make sure they are compatible and can become aligned with each other. God gave us this same principle when He instructed us not to be unequally yoked. (See 2 Cor. 6:14.)

As individual leaders within the Church, we have different spiritual offices that can allow us to strengthen and guide the Body of Christ. These offices are referred to as apostles, prophets, evangelists, pastors, and teachers. The Scripture states that these offices were established for the equipping of the saints in the varied areas of spiritual gifting and to provide direction so as to accomplish the work of the Kingdom. They are designed to work corporately, building the structure and infrastructure in such a way as to meet the needs of the saints and to strengthen the Body of Christ, thereby creating an effective army which will advance the Kingdom of God on the earth.

Act at the Right Time

Being aware of the impact of completing the mission objectives and bringing that vision to fruition requires you to act at the right time. Doing the right thing at the wrong time will wreak havoc within this plan. To remain in line with God's timetable, you must stay in communication with Him through prayer. When you receive a word from God, you receive the hope that you need to keep the vision alive and stay aligned with God's way and His timing. Don't be impatient.

Consider Gideon. From his own lips he declared, "My clan is the weakest in Manasseh, and I am the least in my family." Gideon was hopeless as he hid from his enemies in the winepress. Then an angel imparted hope and vision to him. The angel prophesied to Gideon and called him, "...you mighty man of God." A prophetic word is a word from God that speaks to your potential. It helps you to see beyond yourself and your current circumstances. A prophetic word impacts you with a greater faith capacity so you can receive a greater revelation of who you are to God.

The prophetic word is God speaking directly to our potential and imparting hope to move us toward that potential. Hope causes your faith to rise within you so that your dream can be brought to light and your vision can be brought closer to actualization. "Now faith is the substance of things hoped for, the evidence of things not seen" (Heb. 11:1).

Have a Purpose or Mission Statement

A purpose statement can and should speak volumes about an organization. Your purpose statement is the written expression of *who* you are, *why* you exist, and *what* your organization represents.

The "who" is the team of people within your organization.
The "what" is the mission.
The "why" is the purpose.

For example, a totally profit-driven organization will do everything it can to make a profit. The driving force, which is both the purpose and the mission, will be reflected in the company's hiring of the people who make up their team. Their mission statement, therefore, will be very profit-oriented.

However, if the mission of your business is to be an instrument available to God for the purpose of seeing His will manifested in the earth, then those on your team will be of a totally different caliber than those who are geared toward making a profit. Profits will become a tool to fulfill your mission and purpose instead of being the driving force behind your organization. Your mission statement should read a lot differently than that of a profit-driven organization.

Unfortunately, there are some organizations that have lost sight of their original purpose. They began with the right intentions but got "off track." These companies, which were founded with great purpose, somehow lost sight of the real reason for their existence. Organizations like this often develop a self-serving mission statement which does not allow their people to utilize or maximize their individual gifts and talents.

When the late corporate consultant and father of modern management, Peter Drucker, met with the top executives of the Coca-Cola Company in Atlanta, he realized that they were losing sight of their original purpose. They had become involved in other business ventures, such as the Paramount movie company, that promised more profit but were not part of their original vision. Disturbed by this inconsistency, Drucker asked the top executives, "But what business are you in? What do you do?" In other words, he was asking, "What is your purpose statement?"

Eventually, under the leadership of the C.E.O and chairman, named Roberto Goizueta, they re-established the original vision of the company and rose again to become the great Coca-Cola Company. It required returning to the original vision to get it back on purpose, however. Writing down and keeping the vision before them is like having a life-compass for the entire organization.

The legacy left by Roberto Goizueta to the company is incredible. When he took over Coca-Cola in 1986, the company's value was $4 Billion. Under Goizueta's leadership, the value rose to $150 Billion. That's an increase of more than 3500%. It became the second most valuable corporation in America.

Mr. Robert Woodruff, the original vision holder for the Coca-Cola Company, made a statement that I keep on my desk. I believe it represents the heart of that company and has caused it to become the most recognized brand in the world. Woodruff stated, "There is no limit to what a man can do or where he can go if he doesn't mind who gets the credit"

Jesus said this same thing in another way:

"Yet it shall not be so among you; but whoever desires to become great among, let him be your servant" (Matt. 20:26).

My wife and I have received God's assignment to pastor The Life Center church in Atlanta, Georgia. God gave us a vision, a purpose for establishing this work. Our purpose statement, the very reason we exist, is: "To equip and empower a people for effective Kingdom dominion living to impact their world." Everything we embark upon is spurred by this vision. We try not to engage in any activity that will derail us or distract us from this vision. Our mission is to raise up, train, and empower men and women who will carry on this same vision. These men and women then need to be able to train others who will continue to carry on the purpose here in Atlanta or in any part of the United States or the world to which they are called.

In order to accomplish vision, we must remain on-purpose. Everything we do locally or globally must conform to that vision. We must always ask, "How does that relate to the vision? Does it align with our purpose? What are the objectives that will accomplish that purpose?"

We've designed numerous tools to accomplish our purpose, such as prophetic, schools on team, deliverance, inner healing and prayer/intercession schools. We offer business and Marketplace Ministry training to equip and empower people to hear from God and then fulfill their purpose in life. Most people do not know that they can hear God for themselves. They have simply gone by their feelings or were guided by the opinions of others.

Our mission is "to teach, train, activate, and mature the saints to become a life-changing army in the Kingdom of God." The mission of Life Center Ministries is not to give people fish to live for a day. Our goal has been to teach them how to fish so they can live for a lifetime. Now we have moved to the place where we want to help them to own the fishing businesses. I have recently challenged the church to go a step further. Let's own the fisheries so we can build more Kingdom businesses. This effectively moves the Church into the marketplace.

We need visionary church leaders who will see entering into the marketplace as a Kingdom mission. These leaders will be those who are willing to align their goals and objectives with the purpose of expanding God's Kingdom into the marketplace. Because leaders establish the direction for their followers, set the limits and shape the outcomes, they must also understand and operate according to God's principles.

By providing encouragement and empowerment, these leaders help to establish the corporate vision. Knowing what's essential for future productivity, they will provide the enablement to elevate and build what's needed to accomplish it. By helping channel individuals into corporate cooperation, true leaders help to produce a powerful synergy that will accomplish God's vision for His Body.

Once the vision holder has written down the vision and defined the mission statement, visionary leaders can align themselves and merge together to develop the corporate purpose. Knowing the objectives, visionary leaders can then channel individual visions into productivity for the corporate vision. We must now learn how these visionary leaders act on purpose in the marketplace to produce what will last for eternity.

Marketplace Ministry Action Steps

1. Read again the story of Abram and Sarai in Genesis 16 as they birthed Ishmael.
   • What was God's original vision for Abraham and Sarai?
   • What was the man-vision they followed instead?

2. Have you ever had what looked like a good idea that turned out not to be God's plan? Briefly describe it.

3. What were the consequences of birthing this "Ishmael" in your life?

4. What did Abraham have to do in order to move God's vision back in?

5. Is God asking you to move an "Ishmael" out of your life so He can bring His vision back in?

6. Now read about Abraham's Mount Moriah experience in Genesis 22:1-19.

7. Are you willing to climb your Mount Moriah, kill your vision, die to your dream, and surrender all to God?

8. Complete this profound truth and keep it before you: "Yahweh Jireh, not _____, is your provision."

9. Do you want to go to that higher level in God?

10. Are you willing to be stretched beyond what you are today?

11. Record what God is asking you to do.

CHAPTER 7

Principle 2: Planning

GOD OPERATES THROUGH A PREDESTINED PLAN FOR MANKIND.
HE REVEALS HIS MYSTERIES AND IMPARTS WHAT WE NEED TO US
FROM HIS MASTER PLAN. THEREFORE, PLANNING IS NOT
JUST IMPORTANT, BUT IT IS A VITAL PRINCIPLE GOD HAS
GIVEN TO HIS CREATION.

Have you ever started on a trip, not knowing where you were going or how you were going to get there? Let's suppose you know you will be traveling from Miami to Chicago, and you know that Chicago is north of Miami, so you get in your car and head north. After traveling for a few hours, you find yourself in West Palm Beach, Florida. You are almost out of gas, but you don't have enough money for gas, food, and a place to stay. Eventually the car stalls and you find yourself sitting on the side of the road. A passerby stops to help. He asks, "Are you all right? Are you lost? Where are you going? Is there some way I can help you?"

You respond, "I'm on my way to Chicago, but I guess it's farther away than I thought. My car doesn't have enough gas and I'm out of money!"

The passerby asks, "Where did you start from? Don't you have a map? Didn't you figure out how much money you would need for gas? When are you planning to get to Chicago?"

"Oh, I knew it was north of Miami, so I just started out and headed north. I figured I'd get there eventually."

Of course, such a lack of planning is complete foolishness. Some of us, though, seem to embark on life in that same way. Consequently, we appear to have no real life. We just head blindly and purposelessly into the future as if we're waiting to see what happens to us.

God didn't create us to be mindless travelers along life's journey. He created us to "be fruitful and multiply." Our life on earth counts for eternity. God created and planned the entire universe. He also has productive plans for each and every one of us:

> *"For I know the plans I have for you," declares the LORD, "plans to prosper you and not to harm you, plans to give you hope and a future. Then you will call upon me and come and pray to me, and I will listen to you. You will seek me and find me when you seek me with all your heart." (Jer. 29:11-13, NIV)*

Apprehending this fact enables each of us to find success in our private lives as well as in the marketplace. When we follow God's biblical principles, power flows through the plans He has for us and results in productivity no matter where we are. The Bible says, *"The people who know their God shall be strong, and carry out great exploits"* (Dan. 11:32).

In preceding chapters we established that God is a visionary and a strategic planner who knows the end from the beginning. Reading just the first two chapters of Genesis reveals God's magnificent plan for mankind. From Genesis to Revelation we see God's plan for creation unfolding. We soon discover that God's plan is established but His tactics change according to man's response to Him. Those who come to Him by faith in Christ choose to be part of God's plans.

God's blueprint was laid out in Genesis; therefore, we are not ignorant of our part in His plan. God reveals the ending to us in the Book of Revelation. We can be secure in knowing that God is a strategic planner, and He knows both the beginning and the end. Our job is to stay connected with Him and to function within His plan.

The Importance of Planning

Planning is the rational determination of:
• where you are,
• where you want to go, and
• how you are going to get there.

Planning is a process. It is a process by which an individual or an organization can become what they are purposed by God to be. Planning includes the identification of opportunities and the allocation of resources.

Planning does not eliminate risk, however. What it does is to allow you to take calculated risks. Hebrews 11 is simply a list of risk-takers; it is a summation of those who acted in faith. Operating in faith does require taking risks. Going to the moon, for example, involved great risks and took a great deal of planning. The greater the potential risk, the greater the amount of planning that is needed. The faster you want to get to where you are going, the more greatly detailed your plan must be.

Planning, though, does not take the history of something and just add to it. Rather, strategic planning looks into the future, sees the destination, and then "works" backwards to determine how to get there from where you are when you begin. Hebrews 11:1 tells us, "Now faith is the substance of things hoped for. ..." Hope, in this case, is synonymous with "plan," because you plan for what you hope for.

We need a strategic plan on both personal and organizational levels. We are in such a strategic moment in history that we need to understand that God wants every part of our lives involved in His plan. We are in an accelerated time in history, and the levels of knowledge are increasing at an astronomical rate. We need to keep up and stay aligned with the One who knows the end from the beginning.

Woodrow Wilson said it this way:

"Some people make things happen, some people watch things happen, and some people don't know what is happening."

Strategic planning allows for acceleration and rapid change while minimizing the number of crisis situations that tend to "pop up" along the way. Effective preparation allows the focus to be on crisis prevention rather than on crisis solving. Good planning prevents delays that are caused by "fires," which require us to stop and extinguish them before we can move ahead to the next level.

The Planning Process

The planning process involves addressing four key elements: Vision/Purpose, Market, Provision, and Management. Jesus had all of these elements in place, so His ministry is still going strong today.

1) Vision and Purpose: Every plan must start with a vision and have a clearly defined purpose. The purpose expresses the specific need for your products or services. We know there is a need for people to have a personal relationship with God. Our purpose, then, is to effectively market His product, the Gospel of Jesus Christ, to where the people are, in the marketplace.

2) Marketing: As a marketing specialist, I operate with "the four P's" that are involved in the implementing of any plan: Product, Price,

Promotion, and Place. It is just as important to take time to examine these four points as it is important to have a plan when you visit a bank in order to apply for a loan. You need to go there with a plan. You cannot just say, "God told me I should do this, but I don't know how I am going to accomplish it." I think we know what the outcome would be in such a case.

3) Provision: The planning process also requires that you have adequate provision. Many businesses fail because they lack the capital and do not provide for the cash flow that is needed for success. If you go to a bank to apply for a loan, the loan officer will ask you about the "C's": Collateral, Character, Cash Flow and Credit, before the bank will invest Capital in your business.

4) Management: Building a top management team is a key element in the initial planning stages of any business or ministry. The Lord Jesus secured the service of twelve key people at the very beginning of His Marketplace Ministry. Jim Collins's book, *Good to Great*, points us to the necessity of putting "the right people in the right seats on the bus." Effective management includes placing the right people in the right positions within the organization. Management also needs to plan for on-going training and ways for each person to be able to implement his or her portion of the vision.

It's stunning to hear that 80 percent of the workforce today, both Christian and non-Christian, lack passion for their jobs, but they don't know why this is true or what they can do about it. The "New Employer/Employee Equation Survey" of 7,718 American workers found that:

• Only 45 percent of these workers say they are satisfied with their jobs, of those, only 12 percent say they are extremely satisfied.
• A much lower number actually feel very "engaged" by their jobs.
• Only 20 percent feel very passionate about their jobs; less than 15 percent feel strongly energized by their work.

• Only 31 percent (strongly or moderately) believe that their employer inspires the best in them.

We know there is a calling on every life and a place for each to fill for those who will seek the Lord and trust in Him. A personal relationship with Jesus Christ brings a revelation of who you are in Him and what your purpose or calling is. Once your calling is properly aligned with your career or your assignment, you will have the passion to follow God's plan for your life. Then you will experience fulfillment and success both at home and in the marketplace.

Planning in the Scriptures

The Bible gives us wise counsel about planning. By seeking wisdom from above, we can understand strategic planning from God's perspective. Here are some of God's words about this important subject:

Commit your work to the LORD, and then your plans will succeed. (Prov. 16:3, NLT)

May He give you the desire of your heart and make all your plans succeed. (Ps. 20:4, NIV)

What I have said, that will I bring about; I have planned, that will I do. (Isa. 46:11, NIV)

"For which of you, intending to build a tower, does not sit down first and count the cost, whether he has enough to finish it." (Luke 14:28, NKJV)

"Let all things be done decently and in order." (1 Cor. 14:40, NKJV)

God also gave us biblical examples of planning:

• The Book of Deuteronomy lays out God's plan for building a great and mighty nation through a man named Moses. It is interesting to note that during the forty years these people wandered in the wilderness, God taught them everything they needed to know, from the smallest detail of personal hygiene to running a government. God planned it all out and recorded it for us to study.

• Joseph knew he had a dream from God even though he was wrongfully imprisoned. He went before Pharaoh with the plan that God had given to him.

• In 1 Chronicles 28: 11-19, we read how David gave his son Solomon the plan of all that the Spirit of God had put in his mind for the Temple of the Lord. God did not allow David to build the Temple, but, "All this," said David, "the LORD made me understand in writing, by His hand upon me, all the works of these plans" (1 Chron. 28:19).

• David knew about planning and waiting for a vision to be fulfilled. It took approximately seventeen years of planning and development after the Prophet Samuel laid hands on him before David actually became the King of Israel.

• Solomon knew that to be a good leader he would need to follow in his father's footsteps and know God's master plan. He asked God for discernment and wisdom. Consequently, he was considered to be the wisest man who ever lived and was obviously a great planner.

• Jesus taught about planning and responsibility in the Parable of the Talents. (See Matt. 25.) The first two servants immediately went out and invested their talents. They obviously had a plan. The third servant apparently had no plan. Jesus called him "a slothful investor" because he did nothing with what he had been given.

The Four 'P's' God Reveals to Us in Scripture

Purpose: Every move of God begins with a prophetic declaration of His *purpose*.

Plan: God always has a *plan* and will reveal it to fulfill His *purpose*.

People: Once God's servant starts operating within the *plan*, He brings the *people* who are needed to support that *plan*.

Power: When the right *people* come together, there is a release of the supernatural *power* that is needed to accomplish the task and fulfill God's *purpose*. We call this grace.

Consider how the four 'P's' are revealed in the life of David. As a young shepherd boy, he received a *prophetic* word about the *purpose* of God for his life through Samuel. He was to be a shepherd over Israel in the same way that he had been a shepherd over his father's sheep. Then God began to reveal the *plan* for how this *purpose* would be accomplished. This was a very long process for David, but after his experience at Ziklag, *people* began to seek him and join with him to help fulfill the *purpose* of God for his life. *Power* was then released to make that same shepherd boy, who started out leading a flock of sheep, to become a shepherd, a king, over an entire nation.

The *power* is the part that is lacking in the Body of Christ today. Unfortunately, statistics show us that the number of unwed mothers, the divorce rate, and the level of poverty are nearly the same within the local church body as they are in the worldly community. We have obviously not affected or impacted the world with the supernatural power that God has revealed to us in the Scriptures. We need to be clear with regard to the purpose of the Church, and then we must align ourselves with God's plan so the people can move in power to accomplish it.

Why People Don't Plan and Why They Fail

Aside from ignorance, the reason why most people don't plan is because planning takes time and effort. Planning requires hard work, and sometimes you have to even rework what you've already done. The cost of effective planning is time and energy. Many people feel that the time and energy needed to plan is not really worth the effort.

Others feel that planning won't really make any difference in the final outcome of what they are doing. We need to understand that planning is a God-ordained principle and a very healthy spiritual exercise. The truth is planning is always a rewarding exercise for those who will invest the time and energy that is needed to do so.

Some Christians do not plan because they want to remain "flexible" for God. They believe that planning limits God. They fail to understand that planning is truly a biblical exercise. It provides a place for God to implement all that He has in place for us. Some people even believe planning will confine and constrict them. This is especially true with young entrepreneurs.

Finally, some don't plan because they fear failure. Past experience has convinced them that they are not equipped to move into the future with confidence. The reasons they have failed in the past may be due to a lack of something in their lives. There may have been a lack of vision or lack of wise counselors to help them discover their vision. Perhaps there was a lack of knowing how to follow through with or properly utilize the resources that were available to help them pursue the vision. (See Prov. 15:22, 19:20, and 24:3).

There is one more thing that can cause failure in an otherwise "good plan." When one operates in an "old wineskin," which cannot contain the new thing that God is doing, the plan will eventually fail. Let's move into planning within "the new wineskin."

Planning Within the New Wineskin

Then He [Jesus] spoke a parable to them: "No one puts a piece from a new garment on an old one; otherwise the new makes a tear, and also the piece that was taken out of the new does not match the old. And no one puts new wine into old wineskins; or else the new wine will burst the wineskins and be spilled, and the wineskins will be ruined. But new wine must be put into new wineskins, and both are preserved. And no one, having drunk old wine, immediately desires new; for he says, 'The old is better.'" (Luke 5:36-39)

Every major move of God begins with a "new wineskin." Consider John the Baptist. His sect split apart as soon as Jesus' ministry began. But because John the Baptist understood the principle of the new wineskin, he did not take offense when this happened. In fact, he said, *"He [Jesus] must increase, but I must decrease" (John 3:30)*.

Other vivid demonstrations of God pouring out His new wine into new wineskins include the following: the Day of Pentecost, the Reformation (Luther, Calvin, Zwingli), the Apostolic Reformation (Wagner, Hamon), and, in our present age, Marketplace Ministry.

To understand how the *purpose* and *mission* of Marketplace Ministry is unfolding within the flow of the Apostolic Reformation, read what Peter Wagner of Global Harvest Ministries says about this new move of God:

"The New Apostolic Reformation is an extraordinary work of God at the close of the twentieth century, which is, to a significant extent, changing the shape of Protestant Christianity around the world. For almost 500 years Christian churches have largely functioned within traditional denominational structures of one kind or another. Particularly in the 1990s, but with roots going back for almost a century, new forms and operational procedures began to emerge in areas such as local church government, interchurch relationships, financing, evangelism, missions, prayer, leadership selection and training, the role of supernatural power, worship and other important aspects of church life. Some of these changes are being seen within denominations themselves, but for the most part they are taking the form of loosely structured apostolic networks. In virtually every region of the world, these new apostolic churches constitute the fastest growing segment of Christianity."

God's Purpose: The Family of God

God's purpose, as it is revealed in Genesis 1-2, remains clearly systemic to Marketplace Ministry: to have a family to love, and to live in unity with the Triune God. The family of God refers to the Church (the *ecclesia*), i.e. those who have been called out of the nations of the earth and into God's family for a divine purpose.

This purpose is delineated to us as follows: "Biblical writers used other analogies from the family to describe various aspects of the gospel. To be brought into God's family, the believer must be 'born from above' or 'born again' (John 3:3,5). Because a person has God as his Father, he must realize that other believers are his 'fathers,' 'mothers,' 'brothers,' and 'sisters' (1 Tim 5:1-2). The body of believers known as the church are also referred to as the 'household of God' (Eph 2:19) and the 'household of faith' (Gal 6:10)." *

The Bible also tells us that each member of God's family has been given the gifts of the Spirit. These gifts, coupled with a measure of faith and grace, are to be used to fulfill God's purpose on earth. Paul clearly defines these spiritual gifts in Romans 12, 1 Corinthians 12-14, and Ephesians 4:7-8.

---

* (From *Nelson's Illustrated Bible Dictionary*, 1986, Thomas Nelson Publishers)

Each member of God's family is created in God's own image and likeness. God says of man, "Now nothing that they propose will be withheld from them" (Gen. 11:6). In other words, they will be able to do all that they propose to do. Within each one of us there is as much creativity as we dare to express. The word "image" implies that we are created with the essential nature of God. Therefore, we have the ability to live together as one just as God the Father, God the Son, and God the Holy Spirit do.

It will interest you to be reminded that we all have the same red blood flowing through us regardless of our race, color, or place of origin. God is breaking down the racial walls and every other thing that has separated us for so long. We, as God's family, must make a concerted effort to unite with one another and become one people under Father God.

Our God-ordained purpose is to be creative, to be fruitful, and to multiply, and this is integrated into the very "DNA" of Marketplace Ministry. As we live out this purpose, our mission in Marketplace Ministry is expressed, manifested, and demonstrated in the world around us.

Mission

The prophetic vision of Revelation 11:15-16 becomes the clarion cry of our marketplace mission: "Then the seventh angel sounded: And there were loud voices in heaven, saying, 'The kingdoms of this world have become the kingdoms of our Lord and of His Christ, and He shall reign forever and ever!'"

Our mission as God's people now is to be Kingdom-takers and Kingdom-builders; we are to take authority over everything that is not under God's Rulership and bring it in to God's Kingdom. In saying this I am not advocating for any particular eschatological (end-times) viewpoint. What I am stressing is that God's ultimate mission for

His Kingdom is the penultimate thing. The Kingdom of God begins within us and unfolds as history moves toward its ultimate consummation with the Return of Jesus Christ. Just as we have been saved, are being saved, and will be saved, so the Kingdom of God has been birthed in history in the Church at Pentecost. It is unfolding penultimately through us and is, in part, manifested through Marketplace Ministry. And it will be consummated in history when Jesus returns to earth.

How does this translate theologically and practically in the present? When I use the word "kingdoms," I am referring to all aspects of life, including commerce, business, family, and government. Jesus is the King now, and He is King for eternity. But He will be bodily crowned on earth at His second coming. Notice what the Scripture says: "For in Him [Christ] dwells all the fullness of the Godhead [God] bodily" (Col. 2:9). And we, the Church of Jesus Christ, have been given this fullness in Christ, who is the Head over every power and authority. This truly makes us special and we should rejoice to know this truth. Ephesians 1:9 reads, "Having made known to us the mystery of His will, according to His good pleasure which He purposed in Himself."

The Kingdom

The Kingdom is, first of all, spiritual, and this means that it is birthed by the Spirit. (See John 3.) So it starts within us and so permeates our lives that every area and aspect of our lives is affected by it. As you learn to release this spiritual power on earth, you begin to fulfill the prayer of Jesus to bring forth His Kingdom: *"Your kingdom come. Your will be done on earth as it is in heaven"* (*Matt. 6:10; see also Luke 17: 20-21 and Matt. 6:33*).

So the Church has been established to deliver the kingdoms of the earth (commerce, government, education, family, and business) from the kingdom of darkness and to bring them into the Kingdom of God. (See 1 Cor. 15:28.) It is this Kingdom that Jesus spoke about to the bewildered apostles in Acts 1:3. It is the same Kingdom that Nicodemus sought at great personal risk in John 3:3. The Kingdom of God is not a matter of talk, but it is the power of God that can change lives and work miracles amidst any circumstances. (See 1 Cor. 4: 20.)

The full message of the gospel entails preaching the Kingdom of God as given by Jesus, not based upon personal ambition or local church or denominational goals. (Read John 3: 1-5; Matthew 10: 7-8; Matthew 6: 10; Acts 8:12.)

The Body of Christ, the Church, is made up of diversified, multi-talented, multi-gifted people of all races, colors, and ethnic groups coming together under one God. In this physical world it is impossible for us all to be in one place, under one roof, at the same time, so we meet in the local churches to be encouraged, trained, and empowered. Our mission, though, is one mission. We are to go out and establish the Kingdom of God, His presence, and His domain in every aspect of life.

We are called to form an army that will go out in full force against the kingdom of darkness to fight poverty, despair, and diseases. (See Matt. 11:12-15.) We must break down the functional walls that have separated church and state, to work together for the common good.

Faith-based funding and faith-based initiatives must be taken seriously by the Church. We must also interface and work with businesses as well as government agencies. This is part of the transfer of wealth. Businesses provide the means for financing the required tasks, while the government provides the structure for bringing things together. The Church has the mercy and compassion that are necessary to respond to the needs of the individual.

The Church must also create resources, training, and continuing education for business leaders. This training needs to equip business leaders to think within the biblical ethics of righteousness and justice. Just as the Old Testament prophets spoke directly to the economic and political practices of their day, so must the Church speak today. This may be a difficult concept for traditional thinkers. If we desire the new wine, we must have new wineskins. Let us join with Amos in declaring:

> *They hate the one who rebukes in the gate,*
> *And they abhor the one who speaks uprightly.*
> *Therefore, because you tread down the poor*
> *And take grain taxes from him,*
> *Though you have built houses of hewn stone,*
> *Yet you shall not dwell in them;*
> *You have planted pleasant vineyards,*
> *But you shall not drink wine from them.*
> *For I know your manifold transgressions*
> *And your mighty sins:*
> *Afflicting the just and taking bribes;*
> *Diverting the poor from justice at the gate.*
> *Therefore the prudent keep silent at that time,*
> *For it is an evil time.*
>
> *Seek good and not evil,*
> *That you may live;*
> *So the LORD God of hosts will be with you,*
> *As you have spoken.*
> *Hate evil, love good;*
> *Establish justice in the gate.*
> *It may be that the LORD God of hosts*
> *Will be gracious to the remnant of Joseph.*
>
> *"I hate, I despise your feast days,*
> *And I do not savor your sacred assemblies.*
> *Though you offer Me burnt offerings and your grain*
> *offerings,*
> *I will not accept them,*

Nor will I regard your fattened peace offerings.
Take away from Me the noise of your songs,
For I will not hear the melody of your stringed instruments.
But let justice run down like water,
And righteousness like a mighty stream.
(Amos 5:10-15, 21-24)

The Apostle James spoke of this in his admonishment to those who are rich oppressors. When we do not teach a Kingdom-world view, a perverted view of riches will result. Having riches is not a sin if it is managed for God, but if it manages you, then it is sinful. Wealth is a great servant, but a terrible master.

Thankfully, our God is not a traditional God; He is a vibrant, dynamic God who cannot be caught up in old mind-sets and the dualistic agendas of men. Christianity must not be acculturated. H. Richard Niebuhr wrote in *Christ and Culture*, "At times it is Christ against culture as well as Christ within culture. But Christ is never under culture; He is always over and Lord of culture!"

Man may say we need to separate Church and culture, but the earth belongs to the Lord. (See Ps. 24:1.) God has given dominion over the earth to us. (See Gen. 1-2 and Ps. 115:16.) Government, business, and the Church are all God's ideas, and they are meant to work together under His Lordship in order to fulfill His purpose, which is uniting the family of God.

Purpose for Jesus, the Christ

God is love. His purpose and plan are to have a family, and to be the Father over that family. We have been chosen as vessels or containers for the distribution of God's *agape* love in the earth. As the family of God, we share one heritage—a divine heritage that started with Adam and Eve. We are a family with one vision and one "spiritual DNA," which is to passed on from generation to generation. It was this vision that Jesus held on to in the Garden of Gethsemane. In the face of severe temptation, Jesus was able to choose God's will and purpose for His life, because He saw the greater good. Motivated by love, Jesus gave in to the one family vision of God, and now charges us to do the same.

Ephesians 1: 7-10 and 2:6-10 explains the work of redemption as simply being to make the Father known and to restore us back into His family. God the Father desires to continually shower His love upon His family. Even though we fell short of this privilege and became prodigals, our Father watches, filled with compassion, waiting for us to return to Him. When we do so, He orders the fatted calf to be killed, rings to be placed on our fingers, and a celebration to be held in our honor. (See Luke 15:11-24). This is exactly what Jesus came to show us—the Father's heart. Jesus knew that if we could come to know the Father, we would surely love Him. You cannot know God the Father and not love Him. Jesus came to show us who God the Father really is.

Jesus' purpose on earth was to show us who the Father is and reveal God's unconditional love for us. Right now God loves us with all the love that is within Him. He loves us now as much as He ever will. There is absolutely nothing that we can do to get more of His love.

Jesus says, in John 14:9-11, that anyone who has seen Him has seen the Father. He explains that He is in the Father and the Father is in Him, and that the very words He speaks to us are not His words, but the Father's. In John 17, Jesus prays for His Church to have the same love that He and the Father have had throughout eternity. We were created as objects of His love.

THE CORE MESSAGE OF JESUS: GOD LOVES YOU!

John 20:31 says, " But these are written that you may believe that Jesus is the Christ, the Son of God, and that believing you may have life in His name." Jesus modeled the heart of the Father by showing us all God's attributes.

> *"For God so loved the world that He gave His only begotten Son, that whosoever believes in Him should not perish but have everlasting life" (John 3:16).*

The Mission of Jesus: To Fulfill the Scripture by the Demonstration of the Works of the Messiah.

In Luke 4:18-19, Jesus stood and read from the scroll of the Prophet Isaiah:

> *"The Spirit of the Lord is on me, because He has anointed me to preach good news to the poor. He has sent me to proclaim freedom for the prisoners and recovery of sight for the blind, to release the oppressed, and to proclaim the year of the Lord's favor." (NIV)*

Specifically, the earthly mission of Jesus was to:
• Defeat the enemy—Satan.
• Reveal sin and show us the roots of sin.
• Fulfill the Law.
• Provide a better sacrifice.
• Establish the Church to carry on the work of the ministry after His departure.
• Teach us the principles of the New Covenant, the new wineskin.
• Teach us new attitudes or the Beatitudes. (Read Matt. 5.)

Jesus accomplished His mission so that all limitations could be removed from the Church and to restore all things back to their rightful place. He did these things to demonstrate who the Father is and to reveal the Father's heart to us. When Jesus broke the loaves and fishes and fed the 5000, He was demonstrating that there is no scarcity in God's Kingdom. God the Father does not want us to be anxious about what we need to eat or drink. Jesus healed the lame and the brokenhearted and then He raised the dead. Now each member of the Church is to live and conduct ourselves in such a way that we reflect the Father's heart and demonstrate who He is. Everything we are or do must point to God's character and nature. That is what it means to be a witness. You are to be salt and light in every area of your life, and the marketplace is where you are assigned to do this.

Jesus started His ministry with the twelve disciples. Then there were seventy-two, then 120, then 3000. Today there are over two billion Christians on the face of the earth and the acceleration and momentum continue to climb.

We know that God is not finished yet. We know He is building a much stronger Church, a beautiful bride that will take the full gospel and the full restoration plan to the ends of the earth. We know that His plan is for the earth to be filled with His glory, with Jesus ruling and reigning over the entire universe. We know we are part of that plan.

God's Paradigm of Planning for the Church

The planning paradigm for the Church involves three areas:
• Organization
• Objectives
• Operational Plan

God's Organization—the Church

The Church is God's organization, and it is made up of many called-out members. It is designed to work as a corporate body in order to establish God's vision, purpose, and mission in the earth, using His master plan.

Author and management guru, the late Peter Drucker, tells us that an organization, in general, is defined by the wants of the customer, and it is satisfied when the customer buys the products and/or services. To satisfy the customer is the mission and purpose of every business. Business enterprise, however common, requires that the theory of the business be thought through and spelled out.

- The local church, the organization in this case, is to teach, train, and activate its members to transform a lost and dying world.
- The product is the full message of the Gospel of Jesus Christ, including redemption, restoration, and discipleship for all mankind.
- The business enterprise or organization is the Church. We are workers who must think through and spell out the strategies that have been laid out by Jesus.
- The primary goal is to raise godly communities worldwide that will enroll in the vision of the organization (the Church) so the mission of full redemption can be effectively accomplished.
- The ultimate mission of the Church is to establish the Kingdom of God and to cover the earth with God's glory.

The world is crying out for what we have. We have not yet figured out an effective strategy to market and sell it to them, however. We have withheld the effective influences of the Body of Christ from the world. Jesus told the woman at the well, "I have water that you will never be able to get on your own." As long as the world can duplicate what we have or find a close generic option, people will never "buy" from us. We must present the authentic full message of the gospel in the power of the Holy Sprit in order to dispel all the counterfeits.

God's Objectives

Our objectives are basically the extended objectives of the Lord Jesus:
- To establish the Church through our Christ-given authority.
- To go forth and keep the enemy defeated.

- To go forth and set the captives free in all areas of their lives.
- To show the Father's heart to the world and break down old mind-sets.
- To operate with power through God's Kingdom principles.

> *Then Jesus came to them and said, "All **authority** [Greek: exousia] in heaven and on earth has been given to me. Therefore **go** and **make disciples of all nations, baptizing** them in the name of the Father and of the Son and of the Holy Spirit, and **teaching** them to obey everything I have commanded you. And surely I am with you always, to the very end of the age." (Matt. 28:18-20, NIV, emphasis mine)*

We see these objectives rooted in the Great Commission that is recorded in Matthew 28. The operative imperative of the Great Commission is to "make disciples." This means that, as disciples, we are to reproduce and multiply ourselves. The primary asset in this business is the people (the "customers") who are transformed as a result of being *reached.* Jesus commanded us to *"go"* and meet "the prospective customer" where he or she is—out in the marketplace. We are to "baptize" them or immerse them in Christ so they will be *changed* or *converted* and will become willing to be living sacrifices, as well. Then we are to *train and equip* these new disciples, *teaching* them to put on the mind of Christ and obey God's commands.

Notice the power and authority that God gave to Jesus is foundational to the fulfillment of the Great Commission. The Greek word for power is *exousia,* which means: "the power and authority of right; the power of rule or government" (From *Thayer's Greek Lexicon,* Abridged). So Christ was given delegated authority to be in the business of establishing His Kingdom on earth. He, in turn, gives us delegated authority and power to accomplish His Kingdom objectives.

Fulfilling these objectives by taking His Kingdom into the marketplace arenas of family, businesss, and government, therefore, isn't a suggestion; it's a mandate!

God's Operational Plan

God has a simple management and operational structure which is called the Five-Fold Ministry—apostles, prophets, evangelists, pastors, and teachers. Here's how they are to work:

> *And He Himself gave some to be apostles, some prophets, some evangelists, and some pastors and teachers, for the equipping of the saints for the work of ministry, for the edifying of the body of Christ, till we all come to the unity of the faith and of the knowledge of the Son of God, to a perfect man, to the measure of the stature of the fullness of Christ; that we should no longer be children, tossed to and fro and carried about with every wind of doctrine, by the trickery of men, in the cunning craftiness of deceitful plotting, but, speaking the truth in love, may grow up in all things into Him who is the head—Christ—from whom the whole body, joined and knit together by what every joint supplies, according to the effective working by which every part does its share, causes growth of the body for the edifying of itself in love. (Eph. 4:11-16)*

Notice that the leaders are to work together in unity and love in order to produce people who are equipped to live out truth in a world that is filled with deceit. The fruit of our labor should be whole, mature, productive people who then have a support structure—the Church—available to them. These new disciples then cause growth in the Church body, thus allowing it to penetrate more and more into the world's culture. Now it's time for us to address specifically how the Body of Christ is to operate within God's master plan.

Marketplace Ministry Action Steps

1. Read again this powerful statement about Strategic Planning.
• "Planning does not take the history of something and just add to it. Rather it looks into the future, sees the destination, and then 'works' backwards to determine how to get there."
• Has your planning process been based on past history or your future destination?
• What are you going to do differently now that you have this truth?

2. Woodrow Wilson said, *"Some people make things happen, some people watch things happen, and some people don't know what is happening."*
• What do you have to do to become a person who makes things happen?

3. Review this list of "lacks":
• Lack of vision, lack of wise counsel, lack of knowledge

4. Are any of these "lacks" keeping you from planning for your future?
• If your answer to this question is "yes," what is God telling you to do now?

5. Read Proverbs 15:22, 19:20, and 24:3 to help you with this process.

CHAPTER 8

Principle 3:
Workmanship

GOD WORKS, JESUS WORKS, AND THE HOLY SPIRIT IS WORKING.
THIS IS A PRINCIPLE THAT GOD BEGAN WITH HIS CREATION
AND WILL CONTINUE THROUGHOUT ETERNITY.

W e cannot overemphasize the fact that God is a strategic planner. In the preceding chapters we discussed the vision God has for His Kingdom and His strategic plan to get the work accomplished. We know that God already has a plan that covers everything from the beginning to the end. As we plug into His heart and walk with Him, we too will be able to see the expected conclusion of His plan unfold.

The resounding theme of God's plan is that the current kingdoms of this world will all, in the end, become part of the Kingdom of our Lord. Revelation 11:15 clearly reveals that the expected conclusion of God's plan is that Christ shall reign over everything forever and ever. With this in mind, God proceeded with the work of creation.

Colossians 1:16 tells us: *"For by him all things were created: things in heaven and on earth, visible and invisible...all things were created by him and for him" (NIV).*

God's plan is further revealed to us in Colossians 1:19: "God was pleased to have all his fullness dwell in him, and through him to reconcile to himself all things, whether things on earth or things in heaven, by making peace through his blood, shed on the cross" (NIV). Paul, the writer of this letter, says he was commissioned to reveal "the mystery that has been kept hidden for ages and generations, but is now disclosed to the saints" (Col. 1:26, NIV). That mystery, he explains, is that Christ has a body, the Church, which was from the beginning, and that we are to be one, reconciled to each other and that Christ dwells in us. Therefore, we, the Body of Christ, are to be the examples, and we are to do the work!

Studying God's plan for His Kingdom reveals to us not only the way God thinks but also the way He gets the job done. All of God's plans are built on His principles, which directly reflect His nature and His character. That is why it is vitally important for everyone who participates in God's plan at any level to have a first-hand understanding of God's nature and character vis-à-vis His principles.

Consider why the children of Israel spent forty years in "God's School of Principles" after their deliverance from slavery in Egypt. On their way to occupy Canaan, they had to be taught every principle they would ever need for life in the Kingdom. Having been subject to the bondage of slavery for years, they had to become knowledgeable in the plan of God, ranging from personal responsibility to establishing and running a worldwide government.

How would God use a people who had no prior understanding of government, family, marriage, money, religion, or business to become the means for establishing His Kingdom on the earth? This new nation was the forerunner of the Church, which would have the same God-given purpose. God taught these former slaves what they needed to know concerning His laws under the leadership of Moses. God then had Moses write down each one in the Book of Deuteronomy so they could be passed on to future generations. For my own personal use, I have highlighted in different colors these foundational principles in the Book of Deuteronomy in my study Bible.

Jesus said that He came to fulfill these laws through the one Great Commandment, which is to *love God and love one another.* The laws of the Old Covenant are able to show us when we are in violation of this one Great Commandment. The Apostle Paul said we would not know when we missed the mark if we did not have the Law as the schoolmaster which shows us our sin. God's principles are foundational for each of these laws. So, understanding His principles enables us to better represent His laws and precepts to the world where we live.

The key to understanding God's principles begins with an awareness of His divine order. We see His divine order apparent in all God did from Genesis to the Revelation. Within this divine order is the creation segment in which God made everything and saw that it was good.

PRINCIPLE 1: WORK IS PART OF GOD'S DIVINE ORDER.

With creation preceding formation, we know that God's divine order had us purposed in His mind to be on this earth right at this time for a specific purpose. We are the workmanship of God, uniquely made and peculiar in nature. We were created in the image of God even to the point of having His Spirit within us—a uniqueness that no other part of creation has.

Work was so important to men and to the plan of God that He did not release the rain that would bring forth the food until He created men to work in the Garden.

This is the account of the heavens and the earth when they were created. When the Lord God made the earth and the heavens—and no shrub of the field had yet appeared on the earth and no plant of the field had yet sprung up, for the Lord God had not sent rain on the earth and there was no man to work the ground, but streams came up from the earth and watered the whole surface of the ground. (Genesis 2:4-6, NIV)

In Genesis 1:28 we see that God commissioned man to *work* for Him within this beautiful creation. *"God blessed them and said to them, 'Be fruitful and increase in number; fill the earth and subdue it. Rule over the fish of the sea and the birds of the air and over every living creature that moves on the ground'" (Gen. 1:28, NIV).* The key phrase here is: "God ... said to them." God not only set up His divine order, He gave us a stereotype or model in the Garden of Eden. Here the man and woman were first instructed in this foundational principle of work. It was at the end of the day that He met with them to discuss their work, which was a joy for them. God gave man authority over everything He had created by assigning him both physical and mental work to do: he was to *work the garden and name all the created things* on the earth and in the air.

The Consequence of the Fall: Work Is Not a Curse!

As a result of the Fall, all man's fundamental relationships were significantly changed: his relationships with God, with others, and with creation. We know that each of these relationships went through major adjustments that ultimately affected the four basic structures of every society: family, religion, government, and commerce. Man's ability to navigate, research, discover, and cultivate these four frontiers was adversely affected when Satan moved in to usurp our initial authority. But God's purpose cannot be thwarted, for God knew the end from the beginning and His divine plan was still operating and moving forward.

Connotations of Work

Work is our first ministry. God, the Creator, has created everything that will ever be required for eternity. We are not creators, but we do have a God-given capacity to be creative. We are to take God's creation and creatively work it to its fullness. This is a methodology for

130

revealing and discovering His creation. For example, the potential for the development of the internet was a creation, and humanity has creatively learned to develop this potential and use it. Our basic work purpose on earth is to take what God has provided to bring everything into the fullness of time.

We know that there are no part-time Christians in the Kingdom of God; therefore, we are to be full-time workers for Him, and we are involved in various facets of life. The word "occupation" is synonymous with "vocation," which is the work we have been given to do here on earth. Our work is not our calling, but it is a means for fulfilling that calling. Just as our journey into God's future is not an end within itself; it is the means to fulfill our part in God's dynamic corporate plan.

In previous chapters, we made clear that when your vocation is in line with God's plan, you will have success not only in the Church arena but also in the extended Church, the marketplace. Your destiny is not just about you; it is about you and God coming together to fulfill His call and to establish His Kingdom in the earth.

The Origin of Work

As we look at the origin of work, we see that the word *advodah* (vocation) is also a root word for worship. This would indicate that our vocation (or our work) is to be a form of worship unto Him. When you consider that the time we spend at work could total over 100,000 hours in our lifetimes, work becomes a significant portion of our lives. Can you see that God ordained work as part of His strategic plan and that when we work to serve Him, we also worship Him?

This principle has not been adequately explained, so many Christians have not been "made free" by this truth. Since in our finite body there is a physical limit to how much we can work, many even feel that "work" is a curse. The truth is that work is not part of the curse; it is actually a major part of God's divine plan for our lives both individually and corporately. In fact, it is one of the means for overcoming the curse. The Apostle Paul teaches that we should not eat unless we have worked. In John 17:4 Jesus tells us He had work to complete while He was on earth. Addressing God the Father, Jesus said, "I have brought you glory on earth by completing the work you gave me to do" (NIV). As it has been previously noted, part of His work was to break the curse and to restore all things to Himself.

The majority of congregations have never heard a sermon on work or workmanship even though the Church is called to "prepare the saints to do the *work* of the ministry." A major means of perfecting the saints should include understanding and training in the godly principles of work and workmanship. Many non-Christians excel in their work because they are applying God's principles, unaware that by doing so they bring about productivity and worldly success. God's principles apply to the just and unjust alike, just as the rain falls on the righteous and the unrighteous. However, these divine principles work more effectively in the lives of believers because God can then move His workers from success to significance.

PRINCIPLE 2: WORK IS A TOOL FOR TRANSFORMATION IN THE MARKETPLACE

Work is a tool God uses to move us from one level to the next. Since God's master plan is built on relationships, He places us in the work place to bring us in contact with those we never might have met otherwise. The work place becomes a catalyst for teaching us how to work and how to interact with people of different colors, backgrounds, races, and genders. Within the workplace, we are confronted daily with the need to get along with others while sharing our gifts and talents for a common goal. We must realize, however, that the enemy desires to pervert what is good and turn it into something for wicked uses.

Christianity is the only world religion that has a specific theology of work, so would it surprise you to know that the United States has a work ethic that is based on productivity and charity (giving)? God's principles, based on personal initiative, are the very roots of our free enterprise system. It should not surprise us, therefore, that the enemy constantly tries to bring perversion into this arena.

When the Civil Rights Movement experienced major outbreaks of violence during the sixties, the marketplace was the place where attention to this injustice was brought forth. The results included desegregation of schools and the work place and the marketplace. The Church, to a large extent, was not the catalyst for this change because it was considered to be a social issue rather than a spiritual one. The Church should have realized that this was the time and the place to reach out to each other.

The greatest perversion or lie of the enemy is that the world is an evil place. The Bible clearly states that God loves the world and all of His creation, though He does not use the worldly system, which might also be called "the Babylonian system." The marketplace, in which we work, is to become our place for demonstrating and excelling in the operation of God's principles. We are to be salt and light and this happens as we interact with others and make a difference for God's Kingdom in our marketplace. Jesus told us that the wheat and tares would grow together. (See Matt. 13:24-30). Jesus spent His ministry time in the marketplace–with sinners. The work He did carried Him into all kinds of diverse circumstances.

Be careful, though. Another area of deceit that has entered in through the world system is that our value or worth is all too frequently based on our possessions and our employment. We are not our work. Our value or worth as individuals does not come from our work or from what we have, but it comes solely from who we are in God. The two most common questions we are asked when we meet someone are: "What is your name?" and "What do you do?"

Consider Adam, who was instructed to take dominion over and to manage all the creatures of the earth. Satan tempted him and distracted him from fulfilling his true destiny. In the same way, the enemy will try to shift your focus through wrong attitudes about work and the benefits of work. Your vocation might be to remain at home to care for your children or to be a director of a multi-billion dollar corporation. Whatever the case, your work is always to be conducted as unto the Lord. Rearing godly children is a calling of God just as much as overseeing a large company could be. Every one of us must ask God for grace to be effective and productive in whatever our sphere of influence might be. God has called each of us to rule and reign, to take dominion over and manage our specific area of the earth.

Remember, work may be a four-letter word, but it is not a curse. God has assigned His people to different kinds of work; Some are to be shepherds, builders, cleaners, school teachers, cooks, craftsmen, porters, architects, nurses, gardeners, farmers, artists, or whatever else He has need of. Your work is to be done as unto the Lord. Your attitude is to be that of Jesus whose "meat" was to complete the work the Father had sent Him to do. (See John 4:34.)

Work is meant to have meaning and purpose. In World War II, the Germans would often require their prisoners of war to engage in endless, meaningless, and purposeless activities. For example, the guards might have the prisoners dig a big a hole, take the dirt out, transport it, and pile it at the other end of the camp. Then they would have them begin taking it back in wheelbarrows to refill the hole they had just dug. This is called toil, not work, and it drove many prisoners out of their minds, to the extent that many even committed suicide. Work should have a meaning, a purpose, and a reward to be meaninful. Meaningful work has value and it brings glory to God. This is why many financially successful people do not feel fulfilled. It's because their work has no meaning or purpose to them.

King Solomon, though a great man, lost sight of his purpose and became very cynical; he even went so far as to say that everything in life is vanity or meaningless. Solomon no longer derived joy or pleasure from his work because it no longer brought glory to God. The fulfillment that work brings to us is derived from the glory it brings through us. Work is building character. Work is our assignment.

Remember the rich man, who by his own agenda kept building bigger barns to accommodate his own stuff for his own purposes? (See Luke 12:16-21.) God said to him, "Fool! This night your soul will be required of you; then whose will those things be which you have provided?" (Luke 12:20). The truth is that a barn filled with you and your stuff instead of a barn filled with the Kingdom of God will only bring ruin and failure to its owner. It is God who blesses our work, not we ourselves, and those blessings are to be committed to Kingdom use. (See Deut. 8:18.)

Biblical Characters Who Are Worthy of Emulation

In the Old Testament:

Joseph: No matter in what circumstances Joseph found himself, he was obedient to the rules and purpose of godly workmanship. He was just as obedient to God whether serving in Potiphar's house or in a prison cell. He was a righteous administrator in every situation, and he was eventually appointed to oversee an entire nation. So the next time you find yourself in an uncomfortable situation, do your best to uphold God's principles, reflect His character, and demonstrate His nature. Then you will see His glory revealed through you. God may be using you in a manner that may not be evident to you while you are in the midst of a given situation. It was Joseph's work that caused him to excel in every situation and ultimately become a resource for preserving the children of Israel. Joseph is an example that God cannot move you to your next work assignment until you have completed

135

his purpose for you. After Joseph became the head person under Pharoah, he was able to see how God had strategically moved him into each situation and provided for a means to be released to the next level, although it did not seem so at the time.

Daniel: Another exemplary character in the Old Testament is Daniel, a man of wisdom who had the attitude of a servant. What made him effective as a witness for God in a foreign land was his integrity in the face of opposition and great challenges. Others could find no fault in the quality or excellence of his work.

Nehemiah: This prophet was an administrator par excellence and a type of apostle in the time of the Jews' return from exile. He understood the principles and process of workmanship. His steadfast obedience allowed God to use him to rebuild the broken walls of Jerusalem in just fifty-two days and then restore all things to God's glory. Nehemiah and the men he led had a clear understanding of their vocation and did not lose sight of the purpose for which they were sent to Jerusalem.

Nehemiah was a businessman. He was in effect the Chief of Staff of a foreign king. The quality of his devotion to his assignment gained him great favor with God and man. God was able to use this multi-talented businessman to restore the children of Israel to Jerusalem–a feat requiring the use of all his God-given business skills.

Esther: Esther was a woman God chose to be queen because she willingly yielded herself as an instrument in His plan to save a nation. Her connections to the marketplace allowed her to bring forth God's plans for His people.

In the New Testament:

Lydia: This early businesswoman ran a successful dye business in Philippi. By the time the Apostle Paul arrived there, he had learned how God was using the marketplace as His new wineskin. After Lydia's conversion, her business place became the meeting place of the local church. Her resources, money, facilities, and contacts were of great value in establishing the church in Philippi.

Jesus: Our Lord worked for several years as a carpenter as He was being prepared in the work place for His main assignment on earth. The vast majority of His parables were taken from His experience in the marketplace.

Paul: The Apostle Paul also had a work place experience as a tentmaker and this helped to equip him to fulfill his Marketplace Ministry on earth. It became a tool for God to change his perspective of ministry and provide for his financial independence.

Work as a Prerequisite for the Fulfillment of Purpose

We have discussed in previous chapters God has brought us into eternity present to fulfill our mission, which is connected to our work, our assignment. This is all part of God's master plan – Paul explained it well in his letter to the Church at Ephesus. Ephesians 2:8, 9, 10. For by grace are ye saved through faith; and that not of yourelves: it is the gift of God. Not of works, lest any man should boast. For we are his workmanship, created in Christ Jesus unto good works, which God hath before ordained that we should walk in them.

By closely examining the lives of these biblical characters we see that they were trained first as workers. God promoted them after they had willingly used their giftings to give of themselves in whatever situations God had placed them.

Paul, a tentmaker by vocation, was called to be an apostle, but he became very discouraged when he was not received by the Jewish religious community. Because of his work place interaction with fellow tentmakers, Priscilla and Aquila, Paul began to reach out to communities apart from the Jews. When Paul became bi-vocational through his Marketplace Ministry with Aquila and Priscilla, he was able to fulfill the prophetic calling on his life. His work caused a change in his *modus operandi.* He moved his meetings from the Temple to homes, and this gave him more access to the Gentiles to whom he was called. His work ethics, such as using his own funds, earned him the respect of the Gentiles and drew them to him in the marketplace. Paul used this same model to take the gospel to Asia and into Europe.

We see this model used effectively again when Paul met the successful businesswoman, Lydia, in Philippi. Isn't it interesting how God uses our life experiences and training even though we may not be able to see the connection at the time? Paul, trained as a tentmaker, raised as a Jew, educated as a Pharisee, probably had no expectation of using his trade in his "alternative" work. However, God strategically used his tent making to cause Paul's Kingdom work to move forward in an untraditional manner.

Paul's mission was not primarily to the Jews; it was to the Gentiles. Priscilla and Aquila were strategically positioned by God in the marketplace to steer Paul back onto the course of his destiny. Paul began to have fellowship meetings in the home of this couple, and this opened the door to his worldwide ministry. It took a marketplace alliance to get Paul from the Temple to the marketplace. This changed the whole history of how the gospel would be delivered.

God is now calling the Church to return to this powerful truth. Paul laid down his tent making to become a minister for God only to find out later that his trade was to become a strategic part of his calling. His ministry was to include all of his life experiences; it was not to become compartmentalized or dualistic by separating work from ministry. All of life's experiences are to be redeemed and used for God's glory.

You may have wondered why God would prepare you in ways that you may feel are unusual or even peculiar. In 2 Corinthians 4:18 we are told that the things that are seen are temporal while the unseen things are eternal. What you do in obedience to the Lord in the marketplace, though it may seem to go unnoticed by others, is of seriously eternal significance. In Malachi 3:16 we are told that all the good things we do in the marketplace are being recorded in heaven on God's scroll.

Work in the New Testament Church

In our study of the Bible, we must make an effort to see who and what the writers are addressing and why they are writing. Even though the Bible has a worldwide lifetime application, we must recognize that the writers' perspectives may be based on the particular group of people they were addressing or the prevailing issues of their time. Paul spoke to the Hebrews, Greeks, and Romans at different times throughout his New Testament writings. He used different arguments and different philosophies of life, depending on which group of people he was addressing, but all his teachings were within the context of God's principles.

As we study Paul's teaching on work in the New Testament, we need to know the different groups of people he was addressing. The Greeks, for example, did not like work because they looked at it as something that was not meant for the upper classes. The Greeks considered work to be subservient; therefore, they attached no value to it. The Romans, on the other hand, believed in work, but they believed that all manual work should be done through slaves. Roman officials ran the government and controlled the money, but the slaves were to do the actual physical work.

The Hebrews' idea of work was quite different from that of either the Greeks or the Romans. They believed that work was meaningful to God and, therefore, it was something to be willingly embraced.

Paul kept in mind these opposing cultures as he wrote his epistles. Out of this unique combination of cultures came what has come to be known as "Dualism of Work." Work was on one far side, while religion was on the other, and the two did not come together. Does this sound familiar? Does this sound like our world today? Dualism of work is one of the many worldly principles that have attempted to infiltrate the gospel and adulterate the principles of God. The people from Jesus' hometown did not expect any good thing to come from Him because, as far as they were concerned, He was a "mere carpenter." Remember the question, *"What good can come out Nazareth?"*?

God revealed the great mystery of reconciliation through Christ in Paul's Letter to the Church at Ephesus. After Paul, under the direction of the Holy Spirit, described the great plan and work of God in the first chapter, he skillfully drew attention to our part in all of this. He confirms that we are redeemed "by faith through grace," not only for fellowship with the Father, but to complete our assignment of work on earth. "For we are God's workmanship, created in Christ Jesus to do good works, which God prepared in advance for us to do" (Eph. 2:10, NIV). This is one of the reasons why entitlement programs have experienced limited success. They do not teach the value and purpose of work other than to sustain ourselves. They do not build up or support the mission of the individual.

The Book of Colossians was written to address various issues concerning traditions, customs, and folkways as well as to oppose the Greco-Roman culture of dualism. That is why Paul writes in Colossians 1:15: *"He [Jesus] is the image of the invisible God, the firstborn over all creation."* It was important that these people would know that Jesus was everything the Father was and, above all, not just a carpenter from Nazareth. So, when studying the Scriptures, it is important to know which culture and which group of people the writer was addressing. We find this is especially true as we read concerning the application of God's principles in the marketplace.

The Reformation—Martin Luther

The Reformation that was brought about by Martin Luther actually led us away from the stronghold of dualism. Luther taught that work is a form of worship unto the Lord and a way in which people can come together to build the Kingdom of God. Although dualism may still be a problem for some, we have learned that our effectiveness as salt and light is dependent on our interaction with and within the work place.

The Apostolic Reformation that began in the latter part of the twentieth century will also greatly affect Christianity as a means of further breaking down the mind-set of dualism. The emphasis of this reformation has been on breaking down the dividing walls and creating a church without walls–a church that is effective in the marketplace. The Reformation led by Martin Luther established the *priesthood of the believer*; now the Apostolic Reformation is establishing the *ministry of the believer*. (See Eph. 4:11-13).

In Acts 17:24-26, we are told that God, who is not limited by time or space, places His workers in different places for different reasons. The present move of God is bringing down the idea and practice of dualism as God brings the Church to a new understanding of how our work will enable us to break down any remaining walls. God's people need to understand that their call to serve in the marketplace brings as much glory unto the Lord as another's call to serve in the pulpit might do.

PRINCIPLE 3: WORK IS A PRINCIPLE FOR ETERNITY

Most people do not seem to realize that we will spend eternity on earth. When Jesus returns He will at some point set up His Kingdom on earth, and we will still have work to do. We will not have to fight against the works of the devil anymore, but we will have to know how to work together. Each of us will have a body, a soul, and a spirit, and each of us will have things to do. It is difficult to understand what life would be like without anything for us to do. We are beings who have been created with a desire *to do*.

Jesus spoke to His disciples about ruling over cities, regions, and geographical areas. He also spoke of different levels of responsibility that will be put in place when He returns. We are not called to be on an eternal vacation, but to an eternal vocation. When we get to heaven we will not be spiritual hobos going from cloud to cloud; instead, we will be doing the work of heaven. When we realize that work is a form of worship and was not intended to be a source of stress, but of enjoyment, then it is easy to relate to the principle of eternal work. Therefore, we should embrace work and do it as unto the Lord and watch what He will do as we do so.

As we come to understand that work is about God, that it is for God and it is by God, we realize that it is for the fulfillment of all that He has planned since before creation. Learning this truth causes us to seek Him and to ask, "Lord, how do I fit into your plan?" God can then begin to change our thinking and adjust our agenda so they will come into alignment with His plan. Remember, our work is important to God's purpose in establishing His Kingdom here on earth.

Why Should We Work?

• God modeled it for us and then He commanded us to do the same. (See Exod. 20:8-9.)
• We are called to be ambassadors for God; we have been saved from destruction in order to deliver salt and light by working in the marketplace. (See 2 Cor. 5:18-21.)
• We are His workmanship, created for good works. The Bible says, *"For by grace you have been saved through faith, and that not of yourselves; it is the gift of God, not of works, lest anyone should boast. For we are His **workmanship**, created in Christ Jesus for good works, which God prepared beforehand that we should walk in them"* (Eph. 2:8-10, emphasis mine).

• To build moral discipline and character in us. Much opportunity is presented in the marketplace for the testing of our faith. In an area where sin abounds and temptation is most prevalent, a place where we have ample opportunity to demonstrate how the Christ in us is greater than the influence of the world around us. Often this requires us to exercise our faith prior to seeing God's purpose fulfilled. Exercising faith is the primary prerequisite for experiencing the manifestation of miracles, signs, and wonders. You may ask, "How do I exercise my faith?" The second chapter of the Book of James makes it clear that faith without corresponding works is dead. *"You see that his faith and his actions were working together, and his faith was made complete by what he did" (James 2:22, NIV).*

• We are called to energize and exercise our faith in the marketplace. Exercising our faith and knowing that God is backing us up, must become a daily life-style for us as Christians. The enemy may be like a roaring lion, but our trust is in God. Mark 16:16-20 assures us that God will work with us, confirming His Word by miraculous signs. James is challenging us to exercise that trust when he says, *"Show me your faith without your works, and I will show you my faith by my works" (James 2:18).*

• On a practical level, work:

… is provision for family, other people, and the Kingdom of God.

… is a form of service to the community.

… is a means to improve life and mobility.

… provides meaning and purpose to one's use of time.

On a final note, we must recognize that work is meant not only to prepare us to rule and reign, but to fulfill the entire purpose of God. In this sense God uses our work to prepare us to be a blessing to the ungodly just as He did with Israel. Work is not an end, it is the means to an end. Opportunities will present themselves all through our lives, and our work for Him will continue even after Jesus returns. It does not matter what your theology about work has been, you are going to work throughout eternity. How we care for the provision that has been given to us by God through our work is called stewardship. We will address this vital aspect of Marketplace Ministry in the next chapter.

Marketplace Ministry Action Steps

1. Personalize Acts 17:26-28 by placing your name in the blanks.
• From one man God made every nation of men, that they should inhabit the whole earth; and God determined the times set for _____ and the exact place where _____ should live.
• God did this so that _____ would seek Him and perhaps _____ (would) reach out for Him and _____ (would) find Him, though God is not far from _____.
• For in God _____ lives and _____ moves and _____ has his/her being.

2. Do you believe God has placed you as one of His workers in the right place at the right time for His purpose and plan? _____

3. Do you understand that your calling to serve in the marketplace brings as much glory to the Lord as another's call to serve in the pulpit? _____

4. Go back and read the brief accounts of the lives of Joseph, Daniel, Nehemiah, Esther, and Paul that were given in this chapter.

5. Choose the one whose life most closely demonstrates the trials you have been called to walk through in your life.

6. Look up that character's story in the Bible and read the rest of his/her story. Let it encourage you as you ponder the reason why you were in that circumstance, at that time, and in that place.

7. Write what that experience now means to you in relation to your destiny and God's plan for your life.

CHAPTER 9

Principle 4: Stewardship

STEWARDSHIP IS A PRINCIPLE THAT GOD PUT INTO PLACE
WHEN HE FIRST CREATED MAN IN THE GARDEN.
HE SAID, "LET THEM HAVE DOMINION, BE FRUITFUL, AND
REPRODUCE." HE RELEASED THIS RESPONSIBILITY TO MAN AND
HAS NEVER CHANGED IT.

At the time of this writing, the United States of America has over 50 percent of the world's wealth but only one-seventh of the world's population. We have more affluence and influence than any civilization that has ever existed in the history of man. The United States has more material possessions than any other nation in the world: more cars, more bedrooms, more bathtubs, televisions, and more of anything you can think of. It is also interesting to know that this nation also has more crime, more prisons, more illegitimate children, more stress, and the highest level of debt. Unfortunately, we also have a low education level and the highest percentage of uneducated youths.

How can we have all this wealth and still have all these problems? These problems are actually the symptoms of poor stewardship. We have riches, but we are not operating in the principles of good stewardship. Since President Lyndon Johnson began the "Great Society" in the 1960's, the United States has spent trillions of dollars on social services. Yet we still have the same problems we had when the programs of the Great Society began.

What this has taught us is that the real issues of life do not have to do with how much one has or does not have; the more fundamental question is: what kind of stewards are we over what we have been given? Webster's definition of stewardship is: "*The science that deals with the production, distribution, and consumption of commodities. Stewardship is also the management of the resources that belong to another.*"

In Marketplace Ministry, church leaders must be stewards. In Titus 1:7, the Greek word *oikonomos,* is used to describe a bishop or overseer in the church serving as God's steward. *Oikonomos* means an economist, one who is a manager of a household or an estate. Therefore, a bishop or an overseer in the Church must first be a manager of a business, an estate or a household; he must have proven himself to be able to manage the resources of the Church.

The Responsibility of a Steward

A good steward understands his responsibility is to protect the owner's interests and to see those interests increase in value. So when God releases you to manage assets, He expects you to have better results at the end than when you started. When you operate in proper stewardship, there is never any lack. Not only do you operate in a continuous flow as a good steward, but you also work to increase that flow for the next generation.

Principles of Stewardship

In Marketplace Ministry, there are some foundational principles that operate with regard to solid stewardship:

1) Use it or lose it.
You really don't have a choice about what God has given to you, but you do have a choice concerning what you choose to do with it. You cannot just wait and do nothing, because if you do so, you will

lose it. In Matthew 25:14-28, Jesus taught the Parable of the Talents in which He said that there is no payback for the one who does not use his talents. That which he has been given will be taken away from him. Additionally, he will be punished for his laziness. But if you properly use the talents and resources you are given, and give them to the ones who will use them, the next principle will then apply.

2) Multiply what is entrusted to you—the Seed Principle.

This is called the "seed principle" because if you invest what is entrusted to you (by planting it in good soil), you will get a multiple return; it will not be just a simple return.

Consider what Jesus taught us about this in Mark 4:1-20:

And again He began to teach by the sea. And a great multitude was gathered to Him, so that He got into a boat and sat in it on the sea; and the whole multitude was on the land facing the sea. Then He taught them many things by parables, and said to them in His teaching:

"Listen! Behold, a sower went out to sow. And it happened, as he sowed, that some seed fell by the wayside; and the birds of the air came and devoured it. Some fell on stony ground, where it did not have much earth; and immediately it sprang up because it had no depth of earth. But when the sun was up it was scorched, and because it had no root it withered away. And some seed fell among thorns; and the thorns grew up and choked it, and it yielded no crop. But other seed fell on good ground and yielded a crop that sprang up, increased and produced: some thirtyfold, some sixty, and some a hundred."

And He said to them, "He who has ears to hear, let him hear!"

But when He was alone, those around Him with the twelve asked Him about the parable. And He said to them, "To you it has been given to know the mystery of the kingdom of God; but to those who are outside, all things come in parables, so that, 'Seeing they may see and not perceive, And hearing they may hear and not understand; Lest they should turn, and their sins be forgiven them.'"

And He said to them, "Do you not understand this parable? How then will you understand all the parables? The sower sows the word. And these are the ones by the wayside where the word is sown. When they hear, Satan comes immediately and takes away the word that was sown in their hearts. These likewise are the ones sown on stony ground who, when they hear the word, immediately receive it with gladness; and they have no root in themselves, and so endure only for a time. Afterward, when tribulation or persecution arises for the word's sake, immediately they stumble. Now these are the ones sown among thorns; they are the ones who hear the word, and the cares of this world, the deceitfulness of riches, and the desires for other things entering in choke the word, and it becomes unfruitful. But these are the ones sown on good ground, those who hear the word, accept it, and bear fruit: some thirtyfold, some sixty, and some a hundred."

What ingredients of the Seed Principle can we discern from this parable?

• **A seed must be sown**. You cannot keep a seed forever; you sow it or it goes bad. So whatever seed God has given you and put under your stewardship, whether gifts, talents, assets, or money, was given for you to reinvest, in turn, in the Kingdom of God and to give away. Do not just throw it away, but put it to good use, meeting needs and advancing the Kingdom of God. The more you give away, the more will be multiplied to you. Therefore, your expectation, as you "give away or sow seed," must be for multiplication and increasing returns. The Seed Principle is based on hope and faith. It is true that you must receive to give, but your heart must be to be a giver, to be a sower.

Jesus said, "Give, and it will be given to you: good measure, pressed down, shaken together, and running over, will be put into your bosom [poured into your lap]. For with the same measure that you use, it will be measured back to you" (Luke 6:38).

• **The ground must be good.** Good ground or soil is essential for the maturing of the seed. When we know that God has given us seed to sow, we must immediately begin to pray about where it is to be planted so that the ground will be properly prepared to receive it. The ground or soil must be that which God directs you to plant the seed in. As an example, an orange tree will not grow in Wisconsin soil and certain trees in Wisconsin will not flourish in Florida soil. Just as a fish cannot live outside water, a tree pulled up and left on the sidewalk will not live. A tree needs the proper soil for it to be able to produce after its own kind. Soil or ground where we plant our seed must be able to produce after the vision and purpose God has given to us.

• **Prepare the ground through prayer.** Our hearts are soil that needs to be prepared through prayer. Hard hearts cannot receive God's seed. God wants us to plow the ground of our hearts to make it ready to receive His seed. We must examine ourselves and repent in order to weed our hearts of sin. In Mark 11:24-26, we are also told that holding doubt and unforgiveness in our hearts can prevent a harvest of miracles in our lives.

• **Be forewarned about dangers.** Jesus warned of thorns that may prevent the harvest from taking place. Some of the thorns in our lives may be *worries of this life, deceitfulness of riches, and desire for other things.* These thorns crowd in, taking over the good soil in our lives and preventing the true seed from sprouting. Another warning is given in Galatians 6:7: "A man reaps what he sows." There are two points to be considered here: you cannot sow corn seed expecting to reap coffee; and your harvest is directly proportionate to the amount of seed you sow.

Many Christians wonder why they have not experienced changes in their circumstances even though they have confessed their sins and cried out to God for mercy. The truth is that your sins are forgiven, but you have to work yourself through the old harvest to make room for the new. What you have sown in the past may be bringing forth unpalatable fruit in your life today. As you allow God to work in your heart, the old fruit will give way to the new. Pray for crop failure of the old and multiplication of the new.

How Are We to Be Good Stewards?

We must understand that stewardship isn't ownership. The difference between stewardship and ownership is attachment. Even though you may have a title or a deed to a given piece of property, you must understand that it still belongs to its original Creator. God has a way of detaching us from all that has become an idol in our lives. Anything between God and us is an idol and anything that we become attached to also becomes an idol. God even tested Abraham with his son, Isaac, to prove this principle. God himself gave His own Son, Jesus. By planting Him in the soil of mankind, He was able to reproduce more fruit—a greater crop of believers. This was represented by His being buried for three days, then resurrecting and producing fruit in God's Kingdom.

I am not implying that we should not take claim of something that is rightfully under our possession. But we must understand that all we have, everything, belongs to God and that we are simply His stewards, His managers over whatever it might be. It becomes an attachment when we hold it for our exclusive use and do not see it as God's property to begin with. The Bible says, *"For the earth is the Lord's and the fulness thereof" (Ps. 24:1, KJV).* God has no problem getting money "to us"; the problem may be getting it "through us" to someone or someplace else. The moment we start believing something is ours exclusively, we become so attached to it that not even God can use it. At such a point we have crossed over the line into idolatry.

There are many ways of getting money through us. There are ways other than just giving it away. It can be invested for an ultimate Kingdom purpose. Considering that money is a means of exchange, there are many ways of "exchanging money." Money, combined with your God-given talents, can produce more than just a gift to someone else. I know of a number of successful business people who invest and build businesses in order to supply the Kingdom for greater return. This may be in the form of money, jobs, opportunities, or benefits. I am familiar with some successful business people, for example, who provide aircraft for traveling ministries. Many know how to manage real estate, and they give the income to the Kingdom. Since money is a tool, a good business craftsman can use it to build money "containers" for the Kingdom of God.

We have to be able to immediately let go of anything that God asks of us. God tested Abraham to verify if he was willing to sacrifice Isaac. He was given the ultimate test of stewardship: "Was Abraham more attached to the promise than to the God who made the promise?" Abraham had to be willing to release everything he had unto the Lord. I know this had to be a very difficult time for Abraham. When he did so, then he was ready to move forward in the promise of God and the destiny God had for him, affecting multiplied generations that followed.

Satan, at the time of the Fall of man, was not given ownership of everything. During the temptations of Jesus that are recorded in Luke 4, Satan offered Jesus ownership of the earth, but this was not really his to give. Then he offered Jesus possession of the world, but this was not his to give either. Satan could only really offer Jesus the stewardship or managerial responsibility over those realms.

Satan had been given only leaseholder or stewardship rights. If we are willing to take responsibility and possession, we can "fire" Satan and take back our rightful position as stewards and managers.

Here's a key revelation about responsible stewardship in the Kingdom. The Resurrection of Jesus brought total defeat to the devil.

Jesus "fired" him on the spot and held him up for public display. This is not and never was Satan's world. It is and always has been God's—both heaven and earth. God had given stewardship responsibility to man. Man gave up his stewardship responsibility to the enemy but Jesus has restored it. Now it is the responsibility of the Church, the Body of Christ, to restore everything back to the Headship of the Christ, the rightful owner. We need to know and remember this truth, and we need to be clear and deliberate about it.

An Ultimate Truth About Kingdom Stewardship

There is no scarcity in the Kingdom of God. There is no lack in the Kingdom of God, but there may be a problem with distribution where man is concerned. Things may not be where they are supposed to be. So, when we face situations where things are not where they need to be, we think that there is lack. That's a ploy of the enemy as he tries to make us think there is not enough for all of us. The truth is that everything you will ever need for life was provided by God at creation. Nothing, not one thing, has been left out and not one thing is in short supply. We acquire them through His principles and strategies.

The airwaves by which we now use the internet and all kinds of technological devices have always been there. The wisdom to tap into such realms of technology was held back for a certain period of time. There was oil in the ground, but it was not accessed until it was time for gasoline engines and other hydrocarbon needs. Whatever else God knows we need for the future is already here. We just have to discover how to appropriate His resources when they are released into our hands. How do we know that there is no lack in God's creation? After God finished creating, He said, "It is good!"

Kingdom stewardship for Marketplace Ministry requires us to give, not to possess. In the process of giving, we are sowing or investing into God's purposes. As we receive a bountiful harvest from that first seed, we must then reinvest it in God's Kingdom business. Church stewardship often seems to be more about receiving an offering than about investing Kingdom resources for the purpose of gathering a harvest of souls. Investing current resources creates wealth that enables us to fund future Kingdom investments. Think about it. *Are you merely a giver or are you an investor? Do you live in lack or do you live in ongoing abundance?*

In our Marketplace Ministry, we say the process is like A, B, C. A —God makes the person first; B—He builds the business to express himself in a greater way, and C—He shows how this business (vision) will impact the community, which can be local or worldwide. We also add "D", which is the phase there leadership and reproducing reproducers is taught.

Moving from mere giving to Kingdom investing brings a major paradigm shift to our financial mind-set. Jesus said, *"Do not lay up for yourselves treasures on earth, where moth and rust destroy and where thieves break in and steal; but lay up for yourselves treasures in heaven, where neither moth nor rust destroys and where thieves do not break in and steal" (Matt. 6:19-20).*

Not only are stewardship and investing key marketplace principles, being a servant is essential for working effectively in Marketplace Ministry. Let's now explore what Kingdom stewardship and servanthood are all about.

Years ago when I managed estates for wealthy people, some for whom I managed their assets, came to me and said, "We would like to set up a trust and put money into this trust, but it must have a manager, a steward, a trustee. Will you be the trustee for these funds and assets? We want to set it up for our children's education. We don't want the income in our tax bracket." I agreed and the papers were drawn up to give me full power of attorney, which gave me complete control and full authority over it.

I explained to these people that they could not just spend that money in any way they thought best. Putting the money in trust means you cannot have it back until a period of time passes. It was agreed that I would take whatever I thought was reasonable to pay for my time and direct costs. At the end of the time period, I was to be held accountable for what I did with that money and how well I blessed their children with it. It was a considerable amount, close to a million dollars. My secretary took care of administrative duties and wrote checks to pay for bills from the trust for their children.

One day, I saw my secretary writing a check to herself. When I asked her what she was doing, she told me that she was just "borrowing" the money and that she would pay it back on the next payday. I explained to her that we were only managers of that money; it was not our money, and that what she was doing was known as theft or embezzlement. When God gives us money to be a blessing to His children, and we use it for ourselves, forgetting that it is really His money, then we are committing fraud against God. Knowing God will not bless us if we do not handle His money responsibly. I had the funds audited and let my secretary go.

At the end of the agreed time period, which in this case was ten years, I presented all the books to the owners and let them examine all the transactions. They wanted to see how well I had done—how much I had invested and what return came in from those investments. But, mainly, they wanted to know if their money had served their children well. They were pleased to see that I had taken reasonable charges for my services and needs. They said, "Well done. You have been a good and faithful trustee. You have been faithful over that which we gave to you to handle for the children."

It was my duty to "manage and oversee" the trust. At the end of the term, I turned the funds back over to the owners. I only had the use of the funds, but they expected a return. I acted as trustee over many other such trusts, as well, and in each case I realized I was simply a steward of the funds.

Marketplace Ministry Action Steps

1. As we concluded this chapter we used the word "investment." Read again these last couple of statements:

"As we receive a bountiful harvest from that first seed, we are then to reinvest it in God's Kingdom business. Investing current resources creates wealth to fund future Kingdom investments."

2. Then we asked you to think about two questions. Now you need to answer these questions:

a. Are you merely a giver or are you an investor?

To answer this you must know the difference between the two terms. Define a giver. Define an investor. Now answer the question.

b. Do you live in lack or in ongoing abundance?

After you answer this question go back and look at your answer to the first question. Are the two answers related or connected in any way?

3. Moving from mere giving to Kingdom investing brings a major paradigm shift in our financial mind-set.

a. What has changed about your financial mind-set based on what you've learned from this chapter?

b. How are you going to put these new principles into practice in your life?

c. Write out the steps God has revealed to you for this change process.

d. If God has indicated a time frame for beginning this process, include that with each step.

CHAPTER 10

Principle 5: Servanthood

SERVANTHOOD WAS INSTITUTED WHEN GOD CREATED MAN. HE MADE MAN IN HIS IMAGE AND LIKENESS IN ORDER TO POUR HIS LOVE INTO HIM. HE HAS SERVED MAN FROM THE BEGINNING SO THAT MAN COULD AND WOULD KNOW HOW TO SERVE HIM AND EACH OTHER. THEN HE REINFORCED THIS PRINCIPLE THROUGH THE LIFE OF JESUS ON EARTH. THE PRINCIPLE IS THAT TO BE SUCCESSFUL YOU MUST BECOME A SERVANT.

Some years ago, I preached a message on humility and servanthood. As a text, I had used the example of Jesus washing the feet of His disciples. At the end of the service, as a demonstration, I called the members of the church staff to come to the platform and then I proceeded to wash their feet. This seemed to be an effective demonstration of servanthood.

There was a member of the church in attendance that day who had been so impacted by what he saw that he wanted to use this principle in his business. As the owner of a large corporation that extended over a number of states, he had scheduled the national meeting for his regional managers the following week. It was a very high-level corporate gathering, but as they assembled after dinner on the first day of meetings, he took a basin of water and a towel and then washed the feet of his managers. Obviously, these corporate leaders had never experienced anything like this. It made a tremendous impact on each one of them, as I am sure it must have on the disciples when Jesus washed their feet. The basis of true servanthood is to humble ourselves first, then God can raise us up in due time or season. Relationships are established and built through service to one another.

If you want the very best of what God has for you, you must put aside your outer garment, which represents your pride, in order to serve the Lord. The Lord loves you, and He has demonstrated His love by serving you first. Now you must commit to a lifetime of service to Him. Imagine that—God, the all-powerful Creator of the universe, so loved you that He gave His only Son. The heart of our God is simply to have a relationship with His children so that all are included in His love gift of His Son. As the Bible says, "Whosoever believes in Him shall not perish but have everlasting life." (See John 3:16.)

Your Marketplace Sphere of Influence

One of the definitions of the term "marketplace" is a place where business is transacted. The truth is, however, that the marketplace is really much more than just a place where business is transacted. It is a place where attitudes, values, and ideals are formed, shaped, exchanged, and put forth, influencing society as well as business. It could be stated that a person's major sphere of influence is in their particular marketplace.

That is why it is so important that we understand the marketplace dimension in the moves of God. Wherever we may find ourselves in our marketplace sphere of influence, it is an integral part of God's design to fulfill His purposes and plans for us.

In the beginning, as God commenced the work of creation, the Holy Spirit was hovering over the waters of the deep, apparently waiting to implement the command of God. It is encouraging to know that the Holy Spirit is still hovering over you and your household, waiting to reveal and implement what it is that the Lord desires to bring about in your life. As you align yourself with the principles of God, the Holy Spirit is free to move on your behalf. Know for sure that the Lord, by His Spirit, is forming you, shaping you, and preparing you for that place and time of impact which has been set aside just for you.

In this chapter, we are going to examine *servanthood,* a principle that is vital to success and fulfillment in your marketplace sphere of influence. There is no better preface to this teaching than studying the example Jesus gave to us in John 13:3-5. In this passage we see Jesus and His disciples in the Upper Room on that "Good Friday," just before going to the Garden of Gethsemane. Jesus knew He was about to return to the Father.

Jesus got up from the supper, wrapped His towel around His waist, poured water into a basin, washed His disciples' feet, and then dried their feet with the towel that He had wrapped around Him. This was a function that was normally performed by the servants of the house. Servanthood, at its deepest and most profound level, is simply this: *that the King of the universe would set aside His position as leader and take on the responsibility of a servant and wash His servants' feet. For Him to fulfill His purpose and mission required Him to have this attitude.*

If you understand stewardship, you will prosper in the world; but if you understand the principle of servanthood, you will be fulfilled in the world. Servanthood is positioning yourself so God can fulfill His purposes through you so that you will leave a generational legacy behind. Jesus had completed His earthly ministry and knew He had fulfilled His mission, when He washed His disciples' feet. This act of humility not only made an everlasting impression on His chosen few, but gave them an impartation for greatness. By His act of servanthood, Jesus empowered them to remove any propensity for pride or selfishness and move into humility and unselfish service.

159

This attitude has not been prevalent in American businesses. Most executives do not understand that they have a responsibility not just to make a profit, but to be stewards of the employees and customers to whom they have been assigned. Most managers are more interested in making sure their employees understand the principle of authority than the principle of servanthood.

What is Servanthood?

Webster defines a servant as "one who serves another; one who performs services." Webster's definition of the morpheme "hood" is "a quality or state, as in manhood." *Vine's Bible Dictionary* defines a "servant" as "God, the perfect example being Christ Himself; as a verb, it means to become a slave or servant."

Jesus, our example, became the Servant of righteousness for our sake. So the Lord wants us to understand that we are called to a life of servanthood. *So the question is not whether or not we are to serve, but rather whom or what we are to serve.*

It is one thing to call ourselves a servant but why and who are we serving? The Apostle Paul introduced himself to the Philippians as a bondservant of Jesus Christ. A bondservant is one who is totally sold out to his master. In Jesus' day, a slave, when he was set free, could choose to stay with his master. If he chose to remain with his former master, he would have his ears pierced to signify his commitment to serve the one who had set him free. He was then called a bondservant.

The Attitude of Servanthood

Let this mind be in you which was also in Christ Jesus, who, being in the form of God, did not consider it robbery to be equal with God, but made Himself of no reputation, taking the form of a bondservant, and coming in the likeness of men.

And being found in appearance as a man, He humbled Himself and became obedient to the point of death, even the death of the cross. (Phil. 2:5-8)

When we meditate on this Scripture and then consider what John 1:1 says about the place and position of the Word—even before creation and then during creation—we are overwhelmed. The glory that the One who became Jesus set aside to become a servant to God and mankind, is so radical that it is life-changing.

In Marketplace Ministry, the attitude of leadership is one of servanthood that involves humbling ourselves to be obedient to God. Read 1 Peter 5:5-7. Note in this passage that we are to humble ourselves, and it is the Lord who exalts us:

Likewise you younger people, submit yourselves to your elders. Yes, all of you be submissive to one another, and be clothed with humility, for "God resists the proud, but gives grace to the humble." Therefore humble yourselves under the mighty hand of God, that He may exalt you in due time, casting all your care upon Him, for He cares for you.

To be clothed in humility is to have changed your priorities from self to servant. As a Christian, you have no choice but to serve the Lord Jesus Christ. When you serve the Lord Jesus Christ, His Word becomes your Word as you submit yourself to His leadership and the guidance of the Holy Spirit. Servanthood becomes a life-style of following after the Lord. Jesus stated that when we serve the least of the brethren, we are serving Him. (See Matt. 25:40.)

Human Nature Resists Servanthood

A study that was conducted by psychologist Abraham Maslow determined that there is a hierarchy of human needs. At the lowest level of this hierarchy we find basic physiological needs, the next level deals with safety and security needs, followed by belongingness and love needs, esteem needs, and the highest level—self-realization and self-actualization needs. Man's nature, then, is not to serve, but to be served. Another way of looking at this is that if we realize who we are, then we can have our highest level of needs met. As Maslow continued in his study over many more years, he came to another conclusion—the highest level is actually reached through serving others.

So, if serving others brings the greatest sense of fulfillment to us, why then is servanthood so grossly misunderstood in today's society? Usually those who have a problem with serving are also those who have a problem with authority. They view serving others as an opportunity for others to control them. However, servant leadership is clearly demonstrated as we look at the nature and character of God the Father as they are exemplified in the life and ministry of Jesus, the Son of Man. Not only is God's nature all-powerful, but He is also all-loving. How can these two seemingly opposite attributes function in one Spirit being? Jesus, as a man, demonstrated the love of God and the righteousness of God flowing together in His life and in His ministry. He accepted and loved sinners while still remaining righteous and just before God.

Jesus—Our Example of Servanthood

What attributes did Christ demonstrate that we need to emulate in the marketplace? Consider these:

• *Obedience*: A good servant is obedient to his master. He does what he is told to do.

• *Joyfulness*: A good servant serves joyously. He gives his best because he derives joy through serving. His ultimate pleasure is to serve.

• *Faithfulness*: A good servant serves faithfully. He is there when he is supposed to be and ready to serve wherever he is.

• *Teachable*: A good servant is never satisfied with the status quo. He is always seeking to learn how to better serve those he is called to serve. He anticipates the next step and is proactive in his service. He strives to be ready to serve.

John 3:16 explains that God, motivated by His unconditional love, sent His only begotten Son to serve mankind so that anyone who believes in Him should not perish but have everlasting life. A deeper search of the Scriptures reveals to us that Jesus knew He was to be crucified even before the foundations of the earth. (See Rev. 13:8). Jesus said, "I will" to the Father even when He knew that it would take the ultimate sacrifice to demonstrate the love of the Father to His creation. There is no greater example of servanthood than this.

Now, as the Father has sent Jesus, so has Jesus sent us. The essence of servanthood, beautifully demonstrated by the Father through Jesus, is now to be demonstrated through Jesus' followers—us. Believers are called out to be vessels through which the Father's attribute of servanthood can flow into many other lives. Our limited understanding may make this difficult to grasp, but, as we focus on the life of Jesus, we can clearly see the ultimate demonstration of God's love.

Jesus explains this principle to His disciples in Matthew 20:25-28:

> But Jesus called them to Himself and said, "You know that the rulers of the Gentiles lord it over them, and those who are great exercise authority over them. Yet it shall not be so among you; but whoever desires to become great among you, let him be your servant. And whoever desires to be first among you, let him be your slave—just as the Son of Man did not come to be served, but to serve, and to give His life a ransom for many."

A servant gives his life as a ransom for others. A true servant of Christ understands that his life is no longer in his own hands. In Philippians 2:1-11, Paul writes that we are to have the same attitude as that of Christ. We are instructed by the Lord who sent us to do nothing out of selfish ambition but to do everything in humility, considering others as being better than ourselves. In all situations, being united with Christ, we are to say as He did, "Not my will, but your will be done, O Lord." To understand this depth of servanthood, we need to go back before creation and study God's eternal plan.

God's Eternal Plan of Servanthood

To understand the depths of God's love, we need to take a closer look at His magnificent plan of salvation and redemption. Long before the creation, God predetermined that He would do everything in His power to redeem man from depravity, degeneration, and death. Therefore, this predetermined redemption plan shows us that Jesus was willing to be crucified even before the foundation of the world was ever laid. (See 1 Pet. 1:20.)

This is the same Jesus who is spoken of in John 1: 1-3 as being part of the Godhead, and it is by His power that the entire universe is held in place. Jesus had to set His glory aside, put on the form of a man, and come to earth in order to serve you and me. God the Father loved us so much that He gave himself to us through His Son. The Son came in the form of a servant for the purpose of revealing the true heart of the Father to all mankind.

Before Jesus came to the earth, the Hebrew people knew God as *Jehovah Jireh* and *Jehovah Shamah*—God the Powerful One and God the Creator. He directed the Hebrew children through circumstances. He rewarded them when they were obedient and punished them when they were disobedient, just as one would do when training a child.

When God came to earth in the form of the Son to walk among us, His plan was to motivate us to change our behavior from the inside. Love, not the circumstances of our lives, was to motivate or determine our behavior. Being motivated by love would then give us the ability to serve others. The greatest demonstrations of servanthood come from knowing who you are in Christ and then desiring to be a servant of God to His creation. You become a servant without expectation of notice or appreciation from those who are served. Now let's take this attitude of Christ and insert it into Marketplace Ministry.

Servanthood in Business and the Work Place

Back in sixteenth-century England, King Henry VIII, for personal reasons, decided he no longer wanted to be under the jurisdiction of the Pope. So the king set out to change the rules. Those in disagreement with him were called Puritans, and they withdrew from the the Church of England, causing the Puritan Movement to be birthed. During this time God gave a Quaker family, who were part of this movement, the wisdom to refine iron from iron ore, and this brought about the Industrial Revolution in Europe.

To escape religious persecution, the Quakers migrated to America, and they brought their technological wisdom with them. The Quakers (also known as the Society of Friends) had a reputation for doing business with integrity, and they became known as a serving people. George Fox, the founder of the Quaker Movement said, "I do this because I recognize that there is an internal light in me that needs to shine out, and if I allow myself to take away that which will hinder that light ... by serving others, the light comes forth."

Many major organizations and institutions rose up as a result of the Industrial Revolution, such as the University of Pennsylvania Business School (Wharton School of Finance), Bethlehem Steel, Price Waterhouse, Penn Mutual Insurance, the Pennsylvania School system, and many others. The Quakers contributed much to the attitude of servanthood in the work place.

The point here is that when men have been faithful to serve in their spheres of authority, they have opened the doors for reformation. From the abolition of child labor to many other social changes, such as Martin Luther King's civil rights reforms, God has consistently used a person with a servant's heart to bring about these changes. The men and women involved in these changes are called servant leaders. Servant leaders are successful because they are willing to serve others and their God-given vision in their roles of leadership. Jesus taught and demonstrated this principle throughout His earthly life and ministry. Servant leaders are secure in themselves because of their relationship with the Lord.

We have discovered in management, marketing, and sales that it is always important to serve our customers. It is a proven fact that when we put service to the customer first, the rewards will follow. This is a concept or a theory that must be translated into deeds and actions. However, much of business and commerce still put making a profit over the needs of people and the concept of servanthood is lost in the quest for money. An attitude of servanthood needs to be brought back into the corporate mind-set for there to be success in the marketplace and in business.

Business involves discovering and meeting a need or providing a service. Service must be focused on meeting people's needs. Our vocation is our call to serve God, and we minister to God by serving His people. Success, therefore, is not related to how many servants you have, but it concerns how many people you serve. We choose the mind-set that we will follow.

Jesus emphasized the principle of choice in the Parable of the Unjust Steward. (See Luke 16:1-15). He declared that our choices determine our future, whether we choose to serve ourselves or to serve others. In this parable Jesus declared the following truth, "You cannot serve God and mammon; you must choose the one you will serve." Then He went on to explain how to serve God so that He can meet all our needs. In effect, He was saying, "If you choose to serve God, then you must also choose to seek God first in all your dealings, and then every other good thing you desire shall be added unto you." (See Matt. 6:33). The phrase "every other good thing" represents all those things that the Gentiles were striving to receive. God says that when we learn to serve first, we will surely receive all these things and have all that we need.

Principles of Servanthood in the Marketplace

The servant employee. What does a servant employee look like in the marketplace? The first attribute of such an employee is *humility.* 1 Peter 5:5-6 enjoins us to be submissive to those who are older and "to be clothed with *humility,* for 'God resists the proud, but gives grace to the *humble'*" (italics mine). The word "humble" does not mean "subservient" or "trampled upon." For the Christian it means believing and putting God's Word above your natural response to circumstances.

Next, the *servant employee* does his work as *unto the Lord.* Our serving others demonstrates our love and faithfulness to the Lord. That service is also marked by the quality of industriousness. The servant isn't lazy and he/she doesn't waste time. As a result of acting like Jesus, we are light and salt in the world, and we are witnesses for Christ wherever we serve. In my decades of activities in the marketplace, I have led far more people to the Lord in the workplace than I ever did within the church. I believe this is because I was out where they were, with an attitude of doing my work as unto the Lord.

The *servant employee* in the marketplace is also a faithful steward over what belongs to other people. He/she recognizes that trust has been placed in them to be stewards, to manage and wisely use what has been entrusted to them. This applies to everything, from paper clips to purchase orders and from expense accounts to company property. The servant employee always operates fully within the Golden Rule, which states,

"Do unto others as you would have them do unto you."

167

The servant leader. A servant leader employs what I call The Master's Principle. Perfectly modeled by God through His Son, this principle declares that whosoever wants to be first must first of all be a servant. Even the Son of God/Son of Man did not come to earth to be served but to give His own life as a ransom for many. God modeled this, Jesus delivered it and we, the disciples, are to follow it. (See Mark 10:43-45 and Matt 20:26-28).

The servant leader is God-reliant, not self-reliant. He knows that his ability was given to him by God, and he trusts God in all circumstances to see him through. (See Deut. 8:18-20)

Servant leadership is motivated to serve others selflessly; it is not selfishly motivated. We know that success comes from effectively meeting the needs of others. Many organizations started off helping others but ended up helping themselves. I have worked with many successful business people who began their journeys with a servant's heart but seemed to have lost it as worldly success came to them. *The servant leader* takes responsibility instead of projecting blame, and he/she is willing to work behind the scenes as well as in front of the cameras.

The servant organization is customer-focused and service-focused. Such businesses are also customer-driven. They operate according to an upside-down management style in which case the senior workers of the company have the attitude of serving the junior workers. This clearly makes sense. If you take care of those who take care of you, both will succeed. A servant organization operates with balance and moderation in all things, and it operates according to the biblical truth that is found in Philippians 4:5: *"Let everyone see that you are considerate in all you do" (NLT).*

**How Do Servant Leaders Handle the "5 P's":
People, Profits, Products, Power, and Purpose?**

1) *People* must be considered over profits, process, and products. Luke 16: 9 tells us to use worldly wealth to win people for the Kingdom.

2) *Profits* are important, but profits simply provide the fuel for the tank. Serving, not profits, brings life into the marketplace.

3) *Products* must be priced fairly and made with quality and excellence. America is the greatest nation on the face of the earth today because we have been and are a serving and helping nation. Jesus wants us to realize that His message can also be delivered through products and services.

4) *Power* serves; it doesn't control, manipulate, or intimidate. God has endowed us with gifts and abilities to see growth and productivity for His purpose, not to give us power to abuse or deceive others.

5) *Purpose* asks what God wants and not what "I want." It is selfless, not selfish, and it has an eternal perspective.

Biblical Keys to Servanthood

Five essential keys emerge consistently in the Scriptures concerning servanthood:

1. The last shall be first. (See Matt. 20:26-28 and Mark 10:43-44.) This key is rooted in humility and understands that promotion and position are not the end pursuits of the marketplace—*service is.*

2. Our success must be in God. (See Matt 25:23, Matt 25:40, and John 15:15.) The ultimate employer in the marketplace is God. We serve Him and we do everything as unto Him as we serve others.

3. Promotion comes from God. (See Ps. 75:6-7.) When we promote ourselves, we find ourselves pushing aside and hurting others in the process.

4. The wealth of the wicked is saved for the righteous. (See Prov. 13:22.) Profits that are secured deceitfully never remain in the hands of the deceiver. Thieves may secure a temporary gain, but they will ultimately be stolen by the wicked people they choose as their friends.

5. We are called to rule and reign with Christ. (See Eph. 2:4-10.) The Second Adam restored what the first Adam lost. In Christ, we are to subdue the earth and take dominion. We do this as servant kings who know that greatness comes through humility. (See Phil. 2.) We have the godly power and authority to win others to Christ and use wealth for Kingdom purposes by laying up treasures in heaven.

In days of slavery, especially in the southern United States, there were two kinds of slaves: field slaves and house slaves. The field slaves had a strong taskmaster who watched over them constantly. They were forced to work and were disciplined if they did not do so. On the other hand, there were certain slaves who were trusted and given great liberty. These were the house slaves or personal slaves. They were given the task of running the house. The owner or the master would give them a list of things to do, and then they were left to accomplish these tasks with no taskmaster overseeing them.

As the relationships between these slaves and their masters grew, they became servants to their masters. Often, they were educated and many times they also carried the name of their owner. As time went on, they often became friends to their owner or master. Please note that I am not speaking of the right or wrong of slavery through this illustration, I am only describing what actually took place in history. Jesus wants to be our Friend, a Friend who is closer than a brother. Through this illustration I am pointing out that those slaves with a servant's heart were able to develop a friendship with their masters, and they received their masters' favor.

Abraham and Moses were called "friends of God." If you are a friend of God, He tells you everything He does and then you do everything He tells you, just as Jesus did. (See John 5:19-20.)

Marketplace Ministry begins with serving. Serving isn't the end, but merely the means by which those in Kingdom business become light and salt in the world. People who don't believe in Christ encounter Christ's servants in the marketplace, and they come face-to-face with the Servant King. Through relationship and friendship, marketplace servants can impact our culture just as the early Christians impacted their world.

In fact, those early Christians turned the world upside down, as we read in Acts 17:6: *"These who have turned the world upside down have come here too."*

In Acts 4:32 and 34, we read that the result of serving each other was that there was no lack: *"All the believers were one in heart and mind. No one claimed that any of his possessions was his own, but they shared everything they had. ... There were no needy persons among them. For from time to time those who owned lands or houses sold them, brought the money from the sales"* (NIV).

Now it's time to turn to the integrity that is needed in every marketplace servant. That integrity will be so apparent that marketplace servants will become windows into the Kingdom instead of mirrors of themselves.

Marketplace Ministry Action Steps

1.   Could you be accused by those you work with of *turning the world upside down?*

2.   Do those you work with know that you are a Christian?

3.   Describe a *servant leader* and a *servant employee.*

4.   We are called to be both servant leaders and servant employees. No matter where we live or work, we are leading someone, and we are working for someone.
   • List those you are called to lead, whether in the family, work, or church.
   • List those you are called to serve, whether in the family, work, or church.

5.   Ask God to show you how you can do a better job of representing Him as a servant leader and a servant employee.

6.   Read John 15:1-17.

7.   In your own words, describe what Jesus is saying to you personally in verses 15 and 16 of John 15.

8.   Read Deuteronomy 8:18. What does God want you to remember?

CHAPTER 11

Principle 6:
Ethics and
Integrity

ETHICS IS THE OUTWARD BEHAVIOR OR EXPRESSION THAT IS
MANIFESTED AS WE DEAL WITH OUR FELLOWMAN.
IT IS FUNDAMENTAL TO OUR TESTIMONY AND WITNESS
AS A BELIEVER. ITS ORIGIN IS FOUND IN THE CHARACTER OR
INNER PERSON AND THE VALUE SYSTEM OF THE BELIEVER.
THIS PRINCIPLE FOR SUCCESS MUST BE APPLIED TO THE
OPERATION OF YOUR LIFE AND BUSINESS SO THAT THEY REFLECT
THE CHARACTER OF THE CHRIST, THE CHARACTER THAT HE
MODELED FOR US AS HE LIVED AND MINISTERED ON EARTH.
THE LAW OF FIDELITY MUST BE APPLIED, AS WELL.

There was much evidence in the early 2000's that the United States and the world were in an integrity crisis. There were multiple investigations into marketplace ethics, such as the Arthur Andersen accountants, Adelphia Cable, Enron, Martha Stewart, and many more. We must face the reality that marketplace integrity is not as it should be. If our sole purpose for being in business is the pursuit of riches, we will find that this only produces a meaningless and empty life and leads to compromise with our customers, employees, and suppliers.

Because of these ethical breakdowns, the government has continued to increase the regulations that control business and finance. However, these regulations only treat the symptoms; they do not deal with the root issues, and this has added a layer of overhead to the general cost of doing business. The risk of expensive lawsuits has added another layer to this already high overhead. In addition, the cost of obtaining capital has increased to the extent that investment banking firms and smaller companies that need outside capital cannot afford to seek public capital. You can see how understanding ethics has become an important principle in being successful in the marketplace.

A popular story recounts a meeting that took place at the Edgewater Beach Hotel in Chicago in 1923. Attending this meeting were nine of the richest men in the world at that time: (1) Charles Schwab, president of the world's largest independent steel company; (2) Samuel Insull, president of the world's largest utility company; (3) Howard Hopson, president of the largest gas firm; (4) Arthur Cutten, the greatest wheat speculator; (5) Richard Whitney, President of the New York Stock Exchange; (6) Albert Fall, a member of the cabinet of the President of the United States; (7) Leon Frazier, President of the Bank of International Settlements; (8) Jessie Livermore, the greatest speculator in the stock market; and (9) Ivar Kreuger, head of the company with the most widely distributed securities in the world.

Twenty-five years later, (1) Charles Schwab had died in bankruptcy, having lived on borrowed money for five years before his death. (2) Samuel Insull had died virtually penniless after spending some time as a fugitive from justice. (3) Howard Hopson had gone insane. (4) Arthur Cutten died overseas, broke. (5) Richard Whitney had spent time in Sing-Sing Prison. (6) Albert Fall was released from prison so he could die at home. (7) Leon Fraizer, (8) Jessie Livermore, and (9) Ivar Kreuger each died by committing suicide. Measured by wealth and power, these men had achieved success, at least temporarily. Making a lot of money may be an acceptable goal, but money most assuredly does not guarantee a truly successful life.

Many people think of fame and fortune when they measure success. However, at some point in life, most people come to realize that inner peace and soul-deep satisfaction come not from fame and fortune, but from having lived a life based on integrity and noble character. President Lincoln put it this way: "Honor is better than honors."

At a Congressional Hearing on ethics in July, 2002, Truett Cathy, founder of Chik-Fil-A, quoted Proverbs 22:1: "A good name is more desirable than great riches; to be esteemed is better than silver or gold." In the final analysis, living an honorable life really is more satisfying than fame and fortune. How do you measure success? (Adapted from "Business and Accounting Ethics," Smith and Smith.)

In an essay on accounting ethics, Drs. Katherine T. Smith (a business writer) and L. Murphy Smith (a Texas A&M accounting professor) wrote these observations:

"The twenty-sixth president of the United States, Theodore Roosevelt, said it best: 'To educate a person in mind and not in morals is to educate a menace to society.' More recently, the National Commission on Fraudulent Financial Reporting (Treadway Commission) indicated that curricula should integrate the development of ethical values with the acquisition of knowledge and skills. John C. Burton, dean of the Columbia University Business School, in a speech to the American Accounting Association, stated that the declining influence of social institutions has increased the role educators must play in shaping values. Cal Thomas made the following assessment: 'If we want to produce people who share the values of a democratic culture, they must be taught those values and not be left to acquire them by chance.'"

"Ethics" as a word that is not found in the biblical translations from the Greek and Hebrew. It is purely secular in its etymological roots. However, it represents a set of accepted rules of conduct in a particular group or society based on that society's established value system. Jesus said we are to do unto others as we would have them do unto us. He said we are not to hide our light, our spirituality, under a bushel. We are to be salt and light, agents of change, and examples because of the inward change that God has wrought within us. Jesus said we are to let our light so shine that others will see our good works and give honor to God, who is the Source of our goodness.

Situational ethics and relativism are pervading our society. These result from a man-made standard of ethics that is designed to fit the needs and requirements of a given situation or transaction. The rationale behind such "ethics" is to be fair, to do the "righteous" thing.

But ethics become flawed when they are built on humanistic standards rather than biblical standards.

Some examples of situational ethics and relativism in modern society include:

• A major baby food producer was confronted in America for marketing baby foods that had no nutritional value. They decided to pull the brand out of the American market and ship it to South America to sell, thereby taking advantage of millions of ignorant poor families who had no clue about what they were buying.

• The cigarette companies in America had to pay billions of dollars to help offset the costs faced by cancer victims in America. They decided to seek new markets in China and Russia. Today, they are receiving billions of dollars in revenue in these countries, because these nations have no restrictions on age limits. Therefore, they are selling enough cigarettes in those regions to pay for the billions of dollars in fines in America.

That is situational ethics—doing what you have to do to protect the dollar. But if a person is not conscientious at ten dollars an hour, he will not be conscientious at one hundred dollars per hour either.

I had a long talk with a relative of mine who grows and sells tobacco. I told him I could not grow tobacco, knowing what I know today. His primary motivation was the dollar. It does not matter who gets hurts along the way. We have to do what the principles of God say or we will not succeed, because when "the flood" comes, it will wash it all away.

Ethics–Going Beyond What's Legal

Of course, everyone has a way to rationalize his or her behavior. They might say it is not the money alone. Because of our progressive tax code and complicated legal system in the United States, we have been encouraged to look for any and all "loopholes." Tax avoidance can be good stewardship if it is done in the spirit as well as the letter of the law. If not, it can easily become tax evasion. Someone asked me what the difference is, and I said, "About twenty years!" (I was referring to the potential sentence that a tax evader could receive.) Unfortunately, there are as many people who are guilty of tax evasion in the Church (believers) as there are outside the Church. This is why it is necessary for us to have biblical ethics as one of our principles for Marketplace Ministry.

The subject of ethics is the most prevalent problem we face, and it is the most difficult to deal with. Someone might say, "Well, just do the right thing." This seems easy enough on the surface until we realize the amount of variation there is with regard to the interpretation of "doing the right thing" even among Christians.

Here's a hypothetical example to illustrate this situation: You have a believer working for you who has been a faithful, productive employee. You asked him to sign a no-compete clause years ago when you hired him. Your company starts having trouble, and everyone begins to realize that the company might not "make it." This employee then leaves your company to start his own. A number of "your" customers now want to do business with his new company. Your former employee did not actively solicit these clients; nonetheless, you find yourself wondering if you should sue him. According to the original legal contract, you have a "perfect right" to sue him because he has apparently violated the no-compete clause. The Bible, however, says that we're not to sue another believer.

What might be legal may not always be lawful. This can be explained in its simplest form by considering the fact that it might be legal to sell cigarettes in some countries, but how does this measure up to God's law? Cigarette sales do not line up with God's "plumb line." Therefore, things may line up with the legal system while not lining up with God's "plumb line." These examples deal with the law of fidelity. Another outstanding example relates to abortion. Although abortion is legal in the United States of America, it is definitely not lawful according to the Law of God.

Ethics must include the biblical principle of fidelity, which is derived from Luke 16:10-15. In this passage we learn that the principle of fidelity involves the following:
• Whoever can be trusted with very little can also be trusted with much.
• Whoever is dishonest with very little will also be dishonest with much.
• If you are trustworthy in handling worldly wealth, you can be trusted with the true riches of God's favor.

Ethics must include the examination of one's personal character and reputation according to the biblical standard of integrity. Now let's examine the difference between character and reputation.

Character deals with the inward person. In Hebrew it connotes being "pure in heart" (*leb—the inward person*). The Psalmist (David) entreats God, "Create in me a clean heart, O God" (Ps. 51:10). God is building your character to be conformed to that of Christ. We need a godly character, and it is out of this that a good reputation will come. A tree and its shadow provide us with a good image of this truth in that the tree itself is the essence, but its shadow is the "reputation."

I like what Paul has to say about the qualities that shape and produce godly character within us:

> *Therefore, having been justified by faith, we have peace with God through our Lord Jesus Christ, through whom also we have access by faith into this grace in which we stand, and rejoice in hope of the glory of God. And not only that, but we also glory in tribulations, knowing that tribulation produces perseverance; and perseverance, **character**; and character, hope. Now hope does not disappoint, because the love of God has been poured out in our hearts by the Holy Spirit who was given to us. (Rom. 5:1-5, emphasis mine)*

Notice that hope is a direct result of character. Hope is the prerequisite for faith to be realized. Notice that character is shaped by suffering, not by success; it comes from standing firm, not by waffling; and it is developed by trusting God, not by trusting self. Character produces hope, and it manifests itself in love.

Paul writes,

> *You, my brothers, were called to be free. But do not use your freedom to indulge the sinful nature; rather, serve one another in love. The entire law is summed up in a single command: 'Love your neighbor as yourself.' (Gal. 5:13-14, NIV)*

The final fruit of character isn't marketplace success; it's marketplace servanthood expressing itself through love.

Your *reputation* is about Christ living in you, not about what others think of you. It's about pleasing God, not men. Remember, you are a witness. *Reputation* comes down to what's written about you in the Book of Life, not what's written in your resume or obituary.

The key is to build your character on the biblical principles God has richly given to you. Values, ethics, and integrity form the consistency with which you operate continuously from your character. While reputation is valuable, do not let your reputation become the source of your values. Rather, let your reputation be based on your values, ethics, and integrity.

What Is Integrity?

The Hebrew word (*tom*) for *integrity* means completeness, fullness, and innocence. As we examine the connotation of this important word, we are able to assert that integrity fully permeates every aspect of a person's character. It provides a transparency about character so that your walk and your talk are consistent; in other words, integrity allows you to say, "What you see is what you get," because it assures that your inner person is the same as your outward deportment.

Biblical integrity, as it relates to the marketplace, has these qualities:
• Innocence and purity of heart. (See Gen. 20:5-6.)
• Obeying God's commands. (See 1 Kings 9:4-5.)
• Being steadfastly consistent in righteousness and truth. (See Job 2:3, 4:6, 27:5, 31:6; Ps. 7:8, 25:21.)
• Trusting God, not man. (See Ps. 26:1.)
• Walking the talk. (See Ps. 26:1 and 11.)
• Maintaining face-to-face intimacy with God and being in His presence. (See Ps. 41:12.)
• Shunning perversion. (See Prov. 10:9, 28:6.)
• Remaining faithful and loyal to God and to others, including family, children, and colleagues. (See Prov. 11:3.)
• Guarding one's tongue. (See Prov. 19:1.)
• Being consistent in good works and reverencing God. (See Titus 2:7.)

So, as you can see, integrity is the firm adherence to a biblical code or standard of values. It is the state of being unimpaired. Moral consistency is of paramount importance, no matter what the cost or temptation might be. It relates to the sound adherence to moral and ethical principles, and it relates to moral character.

I have been in commerce for many years, and I have seen dozens and dozens of situations that I could cite as examples in this book. Desperate people will do desperate things in desperate times to get out of desperate situations. For example, they may suddenly change the rules and the principles they once espoused and resolved to live by. They may find excuses and blame other people for their own errors. They will blame the circumstances and situations, such as the economy or the government, rather than admit that they used poor judgment. However, the law of fidelity tells us that if you can be trusted in little and in uncomfortable situations, then you can be trusted with much in any situation. Always remember that godly character is more important than your reputation with men.

Simply stated, the key to integrity involves:
• knowing what you can do and doing it;
• saying what you mean and meaning what you say;
• knowing what you cannot do and not doing it; just because you can doesn't mean you should
• letting your word be your bond; and
• knowing the rules and playing by the rules

Do not just go to church just to hear the Word, but be a doer of the Word you have heard. Not doing what the Bible mandates makes the Bible a book with no more value to you than any book or printed material that you may find on a bookshelf.

There was a very wealthy man who asked me to manage his money, and he was very generous in his comments about my reputation and ability. After meeting with him on several occasions to consider the breadth of his assets and ventures, I realized I could not meet his demands. I realized his money was an extension of himself and it determined his self-value or worth. I explained to him I was honored by his coming to me and that I realized this could be a lucrative opportunity for me, but I would not be able to take on his account. I realized this would be a set-up for failure for me. He became very upset with me and almost vindictive. I am sorry to have to relate to you that when his professional reputation and character was later challenged, he committed suicide in his home, leaving behind two small children. All this has stayed with me through the years since, and I realize that by doing the right thing I was being protected.

A lack of integrity is evident when one knows the rules and plays by them only when it benefits him or her. Integrity, on the other hand, involves playing by the rules all the time, no matter what it costs.

I recall another incident with a Christian man. He and I had participated in a number of ventures together. He had been very popular and was an All-American football player in both high school and college. He went on to play professional football and became an all-pro player. He had a reputation as a "great guy" and a Christian family man. The banks wanted to do business with him. Investors chased him down to do real estate ventures with him. He was a true "winner." He developed a net worth that was in excess of 200 million dollars, and he was highly leveraged. Then the real estate bubble burst, and the economy took a serious reversal. As a result, this man's fortunes changed drastically.

Though he tried to do so, he had great difficulty trying to change his life-style so quickly. He found himself in some very difficult circumstances and eventually was overwhelmed by the pressures he faced. He began to take income from some smaller investments— income that was not really his to take. He called this income "management fees." I am sure he intended to repay these funds, but it ultimately reached a point where he could not pay them back. I talked with the group that had the investment with him. They confirmed that he had breached their trust; consequently, they confronted him and released him. They forgave him the money he had taken and did not prosecute him because of their long-term friendship and past track record. I continued to meet with him in order to try and encourage him. His office went from a plush, downtown location to the local McDonald's. His reputation had gotten him to a good place in life, but the financial pressures he underwent revealed a crack in his integrity. I must hasten to say that not many people could have stood the pressure he went through unless they had had the Holy Spirit to guide them through it.

The Relationship Between Ethics and Integrity in Marketplace Ministry

We judge ourselves by our intentions; others judge us by our behavior. We want God to judge us by our intentions as a result of knowing our hearts. So we cry out to Him and say, "O Lord, you know my heart, and you know that I love you with all my heart. When I get through this situation I will obey you fully by giving tithes and offerings, but in the meantime, let me use those funds on my rent." This type of "prayer" does not impress God at all because it lacks faith. It is impossible to please God without faith. (See Heb. 11:6.) And faith without corresponding obedience and works is dead. (See James 2:17.)

These principles of integrity need to be the foundation for any business relationship we enter into. Our values, ethics, and integrity affect all facets of our lives—religion, business, family, relationships, government, and work. All of these realms of life have their own sets of values and ethics. As Christians, however, we should be setting the standards, as God defines them wherever we find ourselves.

It is believed that we have an integrity crisis in our nation today. Some of the reasons for this crisis are highlighted below:

• *Self-centeredness*: We live in the "Me Generation." In Judges 17:6 we read, "In those days, there was no king in Israel; everyone did *what was right in his own eyes*" (italics mine).

• *Ignorance*: The Gallup Poll says there is no substantial difference between the person who goes to church and the one who doesn't. They both have the same behavioral patterns in the marketplace. Most people seem to believe that they won't be held accountable for wrongdoing if others don't know what they're doing. During a very challenging time in my life, I was made aware that there is a clause in the law that says, "You know or should have known." (In other words, ignorance of the law is no excuse.) This puts the responsibility on each of us to know the principles of God instead of being ignorant of them.

• *Dualism*: There are many who believe that God will judge them primarily on the basis of whether they are a good person or not. Most people keep a mental record—a "balance sheet" of their good, not-so-good, bad, and not-so-bad actions and behaviors. Oftentimes, these balances are based on comparisons to others. They believe if the list of good deeds is longer than the list of bad deeds, they are doing well.

A Christian usually believes he or she must do the best they can. They may witness to someone when the opportunity presents itself. When they sin, they ask forgiveness quickly, and they pray or talk to God everyday.

What, then, does God expect of Christians in the marketplace? In 2 Timothy 2:15 Paul explains, "Be diligent to present yourself approved to God, a worker who does not need to be ashamed, rightly dividing the word of truth." We have to study the Scriptures to understand them and know how to apply them, so that when difficult situations arise, we will know immediately how to respond. The Word in us forms the foundation for our personal integrity.

To understand the spirit of the Law as well as the letter of the Law, we need to study the Beatitudes of Jesus, which are found in Matthew 5:3-12. These beatitudes are attitudes that are for all Christians, at all times, and in all situations—the church, the marketplace, the family, and in leisure situations, as well.

We must also shun apathy, which often results when the blessings of being godly begin to make us comfortable. In Revelation 3:17 we learn about a church that had become wealthy and comfortable, a situation that led them to forget their need for God and neglect their passion for Christ. This was the church of the Laodiceans, and the Lord strongly rebuked them for their apathy.

In Marketplace Ministry we must also avoid all forms of dualism, a philosophy which contends that there is a separation between business and church. The same integrity and ethics that apply to one also apply to the other. We are Christians 24/7 and, therefore, we must reflect our faith in love in both realms at all times.

You will be held accountable when you appear before the Judgment Seat of Christ, not just for what you do on Sunday morning at church, but for what you do every day in your part of the marketplace. The local church has been established to equip, train, and empower you to go forth and possess what is rightfully yours and take back all that the devil has stolen from you. In addition to asking you about the fruit in your family, the Lord is going to ask you, *"What difference did you make in the world Monday through Friday at your work place and in your sphere of influence? How did you use the gifts and resources I gave you during the week, in your part of the marketplace?"*

Live in integrity at all times so that God will ultimately say to you, "Well done, good and faithful *servant!"*

Values, Ethics, and Personality

Some years ago I introduced an investment firm that I been consulting with to a growing company that needed capital. I stated at the time that I could not get involved in the transaction because it would be a conflict of interest for me to do so. My job was simply to make the introduction and then not interfere or make any recommendations to either side. Additionally, I did not want any payment if they did get together. They met together and the investment firm decided to make an investment in the company. For various reasons it did not work out and they eventually lost their investment. I felt bad that I had introduced the two companies, even though the investment firm did not blame me and continued using our company for consulting.

However, I wanted to get to the root of why what appeared to be a good investment turned out to be just the opposite. I met with the principles involved and brought in one of our financial analysis teams to review everything. We made a full report to the investment company. The next morning the primary principle of the investment firm told us, "I have the answer to the problem." We all knew he had "slept on it" and were eager to hear about his revelation. He told us, "The man is a good salesman." We laughed and looked at each other, knowing this was indeed the answer.

In 2005 over $1.8 billion was fraudulently taken from churches in the United States. Some of the best salespeople can be found in our churches and, because the church is an environment of trust, we have to be careful with regard to how we handle a church's finances. In the business world, we have learned that before investing in any company, we must examine the company's values as well as its growth and earning record.

As Christians, we should have pleasing personalities, for we have much to rejoice and give thanks for. We should be people of the Way and people who are on the way. Our personalities should be a reflection of our transformed lives. Unfortunately, however, this is not always the case.

I am always amazed to see that when someone writes a best seller on personal or business success, it is typically based on biblical values. Another amazing fact is that Christians buy the most books. An example of this is a gentleman named Dale Carnegie, who wrote a book titled *How to Win Friends and Influence People*. It was so successful that it launched an enterprise which included Dale Carnegie schools and workshops. When you read this book, you begin to recognize that Carnegie has taken the principles taught in the Bible and put them into common language. This is just one example of many such books that are available in the marketplace today.

This is because Jesus and His teachings are central to the development of Western civilization. Over the years, my personal view of Jesus has undergone many changes. I initially saw Him as a stern, serious person who bordered on being harsh, especially in His relationship with His disciples. As time has passed and I have developed a true friendship with Him, I now see Him as having a fun, loving personality with a great sense of humor. I even see Him as a person who enjoys a good laugh, even laughing so hard that He throws His head back while responding to good humor. This has changed the way I see Him responding to His disciples and the way I perceive Him saying things to them. Likewise, it has changed the way I perceive Him responding to me. The Lord Jesus has a winsome and wonderful personality

A good personality should be the expression of the security we have from knowing Jesus and living by the values and ethics that are contained within God's Word.

Marketplace Ministry Action Steps

1. Read 2 Timothy 2:15.
• What does this Scripture tell us to do?
• Think of a difficult situation in your life that you feel you did not know how to handle or respond to.
• Find a Scripture that will help to prepare you to be able to handle a similar situation in the future.

2.   Read the Beatitudes of Jesus in Matthew 5:3-12.
• List the attitudes that Jesus says are for all Christians, at all times, and in all situations.

3.   Apathy results when the blessings of being godly begin to make us too comfortable.
• Read Revelation 3:14-17. What did Jesus say He was going to do with this church?
• Have you forgotten your need of God or neglected your passion for Christ in any area of your life?

4.   In Marketplace Ministry we must avoid the dualism, which contends that there is a separation between business and church. The same integrity and ethics that apply to one also apply to the other. We are Christians 24/7 and, therefore, our actions and behavior in both realms should be the same.
• Are your ethics the same Monday through Friday at work as they are on Sunday?
• Are your ethics the same when you are out with your friends on Friday or Saturday nights as they are on Sundays with other Christians?

4.   You will be held accountable when you appear before the Judgment Seat of Christ not only for what you do on Sunday morning at church, but also for what you do every day in your part of the marketplace.
• How would you answer the Lord if He asked, *"What difference did you make in the world Monday through Friday at your work place and in your sphere of influence?"*
• How would you like to be able to answer it?
• What do you have to do so you can answer it in the way you would like to when the Lord does eventually ask you this important question?

CHAPTER 12

Principle 7: Hearing God

BEFORE ANYTHING CAN BE ACCOMPLISHED ON EARTH,
IT MUST FIRST BE RELEASED BY A WORD FROM GOD;
THEREFORE, IS IT NOT ONLY IMPORTANT TO HEAR GOD,
BUT HEARING GOD IS A PRINCIPLE OF GOD.

God has many words to speak to us. Ever since creation, He has wanted to communicate with us, not be distant from us. When God speaks, His Word brings forth change. When He spoke creation forth, everything came into being. Then he gave Adam and Eve the command to rule over His creation.

"Let them rule" is still His command for humanity today. In order for us to know how to rule as stewards over God's creation, we need to hear from Him and then, through faith, we need to put His Word into effect. God can operate His will and produce outside of man, but He will not to do so. Man would try to manage the whole earth without God, but he cannot do so. God deliberately set it up that way from the beginning. When Jesus came, He restored the authority, then released the responsibility of "occupying" to His Body, the Church, us. When God communicates His Word to us, it is our responsibility to perform it. God's plans are in heaven and He desires for them to be performed on earth. Jesus prayed, "Thy kingdom come on earth as it is in heaven" and "Thy will be done on earth as it is in heaven."

In Isaiah 55:11, the Lord declares, "So is my word that goes out from my mouth: It will not return to me empty, but will accomplish what I desire and achieve the purpose for which I sent it" (NIV).

This explains why success can be defined according to biblical principles. Although Madison Avenue may define success as being one's ability to buy things and stresses the size of what one buys, true success is actually the progressive achievement of a worthwhile goal.

The Apostle Paul, in Philippians 3:7-11, equates success with contentment that is based upon achieving a lifetime goal, no matter what the circumstances may be. I need to be able to say with the Apostle Paul, *"I know how to live on almost nothing or with everything. I have learned the secret of living in every situation, whether it is with a full stomach or empty, with plenty or little. For I can do everything with the help of Christ who gives me the strength I need" (Phil. 4:12-13, NLT).*

Paul, in saying this, understood what success was in the world. Paul had come from a wealthy family and was well-educated, having been taught and mentored by Gamaliel, a chief Pharisee and rabbi. Paul was also born a Roman citizen, which allowed him to enjoy certain benefits and privileges in that society. He had also become a very skilled business person. Hearing the voice of Christ on the road to Damascus had deafened the "voice" that was calling for his personal success.

The voice of the Lord changed Saul of Tarsus. When Paul heard the voice of the Lord and after his encounter with the Lord, Paul's mind-set about success underwent a radical change. He now saw the world in a completely new light. In fact, after his Damascus road experience, he was called to pursue those he had been persecuting. He said he now considered all that he used to have, used to do, and used to be as rubbish compared to knowing Christ. Paul essentially said that knowing Christ is true success:

Yet indeed I also count all things loss for the excellence of the knowledge of Christ Jesus my Lord, for whom I have suffered the loss of all things, and count them as rubbish, that I may gain Christ and be found in Him, not having my own righteousness, which is from the law, but that which is through faith in Christ, the righteousness which is from God by faith; that I may know Him and the power of His resurrection, and the fellowship of His sufferings, being conformed to His death, if, by any means, I may attain to the resurrection from the dead.

Not that I have already attained, or am already perfected; but I press on, that I may lay hold of that for which Christ Jesus has also laid hold of me. Brethren, I do not count myself to have apprehended; but one thing I do, forgetting those things which are behind and reaching forward to those things which are ahead, I press toward the goal for the prize of the upward call of God in Christ Jesus (Phil. 3:8-14).

When we approach life from this biblical perspective all those other things that we consider as markers of success will come to us. (See Matt. 6:33.) While it's okay to have emblems and credentials from our work in the marketplace, it is not okay to seek them first.

Matthew 6:24 reveals that you cannot serve two masters. Either you will hate one and love the other or you will be devoted to one and despise the other. Therefore, we have to decide on what success means to us in order to pursue it. This book, as you know by now, is written from a biblical perspective and embraces the foundational idea that to know and follow Christ is to know and experience success.

You might ask, "How can we know Him?" We know Him by His Word, which tells us that faith comes by hearing His Word. Once we know His principles from His Word and apply them to our lives, we are guaranteed success in everything we do, no matter in what sphere or circumstances we may find ourselves. God tells Joshua (and us) how to succeed as a leader:

*"Do not let this Book of the Law depart from your mouth;
meditate on it day and night, so that you would be careful to
do everything written in it. Then you will be prosperous and
successful"* (Joshua 1:8, NIV).

We also know that Jesus came to reconcile us to the Father. This
reveals to us the truth that success comes from knowing the Father.
As a matter of fact, the level of our success is determined by how
much we allow God's influence to permeate in and through our lives.

Partnering With God

In previous chapters we established the truth that we are co-
laborers with Christ; therefore, we have a part, and God has a part.
We must take responsibility for our part, which is serving Him and
being good stewards over what He has entrusted to us. If we try to
do it all, we will walk in error or in arrogance, for we must allow
Him to do His part in completing the equation. Though we are
partners with God, He is ever the Senior Partner in this relationship.

When this partnership is balanced, God is able to do exceedingly
abundantly above all that we ask or think, according to the power
that works within us. (See 1 Cor. 2:8-9 and Eph. 3:20; 1:19). The power
these verses refer to is the result of co-laboring with Christ. It is this
co-laboring that brings about breakthroughs and produces fruit even
when we least expect it. To be fruitful is to be successful. Real success
does not come without fruitfulness, for what does it profit a man to
gain the whole world and lose his soul? (See Mark 8:36.)

Success is also associated with generosity. Proverbs 11:24-25 says,
*"One man gives freely, yet gains even more; another withholds unduly,
but comes to poverty. A generous man will prosper; he who refreshes
others will himself be refreshed"* (NIV).

Our conclusion is that real success comes by knowing God and abiding by His principles. There are two dimensions involved in accomplishing this:

1) Meditating on His written Word and
2) Listening to the voice of His Spirit.

God Is a Communicator

PRINCIPLE: GOD BEGINS ALL THINGS THROUGH HIS DIRECTIVE WORD.

A foundational perspective on communication is found in the Book of Genesis, which tells us that in the beginning God spoke and creation came into being. There is ample evidence in both the Old and New Testaments to support this truth.

God's communication with His creation was not limited to Adam and Eve. He continued to speak with successive generations after them. Genesis 4: 9 records that the Lord spoke to Cain when He asked, "Where is your brother Abel?"

Jesus described His relationship to His followers as being like the relationship between a shepherd and his sheep. Let's take a look at how He defines communication with His "sheep" in His own words:

> The watchman opens the gate for him, and the sheep listen to his voice. He calls his own sheep by name and leads them out. When he has brought out all his own, he goes on ahead of them, and his sheep follow him because they know his voice. But they will never follow a stranger; in fact, they will run away from him because they do not recognize a stranger's voice.... I have other sheep that are not of this sheep pen. I must bring them also. They too will listen to my voice, and

there shall be one flock and one shepherd. (John 10:3-5 and 16, NIV)

God still speaks today, but are we listening? Let me reiterate that every successful endeavor is based on a directive Word from God, that is, the wisdom of God. (See 1 Cor. 1:30.) A close examination of the eleventh chapter of the Book of Hebrews shows many men and women with whom God communicated His perfect will. We see Enoch who was commended by God and Noah who was warned by God. Also there was Abraham who was directed by God to go to a different country. God continues to speak to His children by the millions. So let us examine how God speaks to us in this present day.

How Does God Speak to Us?

Through His Son: Read Hebrews 1:1-4 and John 1:1-18. We know that Jesus was with God in the beginning, because we know He is the complete or full Word (*logos*). He made everything there is, and there is absolutely nothing that has been made apart from Him. He is the Light that brightens our darkness. God, having sent His Son, His appointed heir of all things and our great High Priest, now speaks to us primarily through the revelation of Jesus Christ. Jesus represents both visibly and verbally, all the thoughts, the words, the principles, the plans, the pattern of living, as well as the character and nature of God.

So if you want to know God, look at Jesus. He is the complete theology and the full demonstration of the love of the Father. That is why Jesus prayed (in John 17) that we might know the Father just as He (Jesus) knows Him. Prior to Jesus' coming, we knew God as the Creator, but not as our Father. So if you want to know God, get a revelation of Jesus.

Through *Logos* and *Rhema* Words: Read John 1 and Romans 10. Most people view God not as a loving Father who wants to wrap His loving arms around them, but as a God with a big leash in His hand,

One who is ready to lash out at them as soon as they make a mistake. The truth or revelation of who God is becomes evident when the written Word comes alive in us (*rhema*). Then we begin to see God as a Father who wants to communicate with His children.

Some people teach you can only hear God through His written word, the bible. God speaks in many ways. The Bible gives us directive words. We can read a scripture many times and it will not speak specifically to us. Then, under certain times and circumstances, the very scripture comes 'alive" to us and we know it is a 'now' word. This is when the logos becomes rhema to us. God speaks in many ways, as I explained, but in all of these ways, they will not contradict the Bible and align with its principles.

Through the Holy Spirit: Read John 14:15-27, John 16:5-16, Acts 1:8, and Acts 2:1-4.) At Pentecost, there was a release of the Holy Spirit with the evidence of speaking in tongues. Jesus reinforces this by stating that the Holy Spirit is the Spirit of truth who will guide us into everything that the Father has for us. (See 1 Cor. 2:8-10). When we do not know how to pray or what to pray, the Spirit will make intercession for us. He will speak through us. (See Rom. 8:26.)

Through the Gifts of the Holy Spirit: Read Acts 13. We see the Holy Spirit speaking through man by the setting apart of Paul and Barnabas for the work of ministry.

Through God's Prophetic Word: Read Genesis 1:28. In this verse we see God himself prophesying to man concerning mankind's destiny on earth by saying, "Be fruitful, be blessed, and increase in number."

In my own testimony, Mary and I were called out in a conference by Prophet Bill Hamon. He has been recognized as a present day Prophet and has brought God's prophetic word to many thousands. It was through him that God instructed us that we were to dissolve my business and start or plant a church in Dunwoody, Georgia. This was a very directive word. A life-changing word, since we knew little of starting a new church. Because I believed it was a word from God, it has completely changed and redirected our lives.

Through God's Servants: Read 1 Timothy 1:18-19. Paul was a mentor and a father-figure for Timothy. Paul instructed his son-in-the-faith with regard to how to bring order to the church at Ephesus. Paul also encouraged this young pastor by reminding him, "Timothy, my son, I give you this instruction in keeping with the prophecies once made about you, so that by following them you may fight the good fight of faith" (NIV). God speaks prophetically to us through His saints, servants, and anointed ministers. The Church must be careful not to reject such prophecies, for such rejection will shipwreck our faith.

Through the Prophetic: Dreams and Interpretations. Joseph had a government job as overseer of the prison where he interpreted the dreams of the cupbearer and the baker. This moved him eventually to interpret the dream of Pharaoh. His gifting influenced the economic outcome for Egypt and other nations.

Through Signs, Visions, and Dreams: Daniel, through the favor of God, gained great influence in the Babylonian Kingdom. He was able to affect governments and kingdoms through his interpretation of dreams for Nebuchadnezzar, the ruling king of Babylon at that time. Daniel was such a man of integrity that his accusers could find no fault in him. He was able to influence different kings through this God-given gift.

Through Angelic Visitation and Prophecy: Gideon, as he was hiding in the winepress, had an angelic visitation. From this, he received a series of directive words, plans, and strategies which led to a great military victory for Israel.

Through Prophetic Counsel—a Sense of Knowing: Deborah, a judge of Israel, gave prophetic counsel to Barak about who would receive credit for the victory. This victory gave a growing strength to the army of Israel against the Canaanite King Jabin. Another example was David at Ziglag. The circumstances were overwhelming to him and his men. When everything was going wrong, the Bible says that David encouraged himself in God. (See 1 Sam. 30:6.) David had resolved in his spirit man that "God was God" and thereby he was able to encourage himself.

Through a Direct Word of the Lord: As the result of a direct word of the Lord, Elijah was able to close up the heavens, resulting in climatic and agricultural conditions being supernaturally affected.

Through Seeing in the Spirit: In the Spirit Jesus saw Nathaniel under a fig tree prior to meeting him. Jesus' identification of him brought faith to Nathaniel and caused him to identify who Jesus was. He then became a follower of Jesus.

Through Servants of the Lord: Other servants of God through whom He has spoken include John the Baptist, who announced that Jesus would be coming. God gave us the prophetic Book of Revelation through His servant John who wrote down his vision from a prison on the Isle of Patmos. God has provided other gifted teachers and preachers in the Church throughout its history. (See Rom. 10:14.)

Through Angels: Read Luke 1 and 2. An angel spoke to both Mary and Joseph concerning the Son whose name would be Jesus. Also, we know that an angel spoke to Jesus. Abraham, the father of faith, also received messages from angels concerning the promise of a son named Isaac.

Through Dreams and Visions: Read Acts 10. Simon Peter was spoken to by God through visions and dreams concerning the way the Jewish people were to approach the Gentiles. The message of this vision was so important that it caused a major paradigm shift for the entire Christian community in that day. The whole thing climaxed in Acts 15 when it was concluded that it was not necessary for new believers to convert to the Jewish religion in order to become

Christians. At times, God would speak through visions to make things so clear and demonstrative that people couldn't "reason" them away.

Through Circumstances: God also speaks through circumstances in our lives; we see examples of this in the lives of Elijah, when he was running from Jezebel and John the Baptist, when he was in prison. Has God been speaking to you through your finances? Has He been closing old doors and opening new ones? This could be your signal for a change in direction. We know that the Prophet Balaam received a word from his donkey. If God can speak through a donkey, He can certainly speak through us.

Through Silence: That God often speaks to His children through silence is particularly true when one goes through a time of testing and says, "But where are you, O God?" Even in the natural, teachers don't speak when you are taking a test. It is all-quiet in the classroom when a test in going on. The same applies in our spiritual growth and development in God. In the midst of a test that has been orchestrated in heaven, it often seems as if the heavens are quiet. Know that during such times, however, there is a great cloud of witnesses who are watching closely with the hope that you will pass the test and go to the next level. God speaks volumes through silence.

Preparing to Hear God's Voice

How do you hear God's voice? You hear His voice by learning to be sensitive to His voice.

• *Keep a listening ear:* Jesus often said that those who have ears should listen. He obviously was not speaking of natural ears. Do not wait until you get in trouble; do not wait until things get drastic and you become desperate to hear from God. Keep your ears sensitive toward God and His voice, because He will speak to you, oftentimes, in the most unexpected places, at the most unexpected times. You may see hear Him speaking through a vivid demonstration of His power or hear His voice as it is spoken through angels. God will choose the means. The challenge is for you is to keep *a listening ear.*

• *Get in the habit of quickly confessing your sins and forgiving others:* Don't take time to think about a wrong that you have committed or someone else has committed against you and stew over it. Let an attitude of forgiveness become a habit; quickly ask God for forgiveness, seek forgiveness from others, forgive others, and forgive yourself, as well.

• *Ask God to continuously cleanse you from all unrighteous personal motives and desires.* (See 1 John 1:9.)

• *Constantly ask the Lord to circumcise your heart.* Desire to remain humble and to keep a servant attitude at all times.

You might receive prophetic words that seem very general to you. It has been my experience, as you continue to receive prophecy and learn to hear from God, you will become familiar with His voice to the extent that you will be able to discern specific words for specific situations in your life and the lives of others.

Recognizing the Voice of God

Jesus said, "My sheep hear My voice" (John 10:27). The question, then, is how do we become one of His sheep? Jesus taught Nicodemus about this in John 3:7-8:

> *"Do not marvel that I said to you, 'You must be born again.' The wind blows where it wishes, and you hear the sound of it, but cannot tell where it comes from or where it goes. So is everyone who is born of the Spirit."*

Like Nicodemus, many people are confused about what it means to be born again. Does it mean that one has to go back into his mother's womb? Jesus explains that you cannot *see* the Kingdom of God until you are born-again. You have to *see* the Kingdom before you can move into it. The prerequisite for *seeing* the Kingdom is to be born naturally and then spiritually. Afterwards, the voice of the Lord begins to direct you and lead you into the Kingdom as if His voice were a blowing wind. Being saved is not the end of the journey; it's the beginning. It is actually the beginning of being able to see, hear, and move into the Kingdom. In the same way that there are things, such as the "cares of this world, deceitfulness, riches, and worry" that prevent seeds of faith from growing, there are things that block our ability to hear God, as well.

Sometimes we are not sure, but at other times we know that we know that we know that we are hearing the voice of the Lord. Our duty at these times is to fully obey and comply with His directives. We do have spiritual senses. Hebrews 5:14 declares, "Solid food belongs to those who are of full age, that is, those who by reason of use have their senses exercised to discern both good and evil." We must learn to distinguish between the voices we hear in order to know which voice is God's.

Jesus has instructed us that the more we listen to His voice, the more we will recognize it. There are always other voices that are trying to distract or disturb us. In the business arena, for instance, we have been inundated with data. We now have such sophisticated electronics and information systems that we can find great amounts of data at the touch of a button. This can be of great value, but it is not a substitute for the One who is the Creator of all of this information. I am also convinced that most people, when not trained to hear God, will listen to their own minds or thoughts and think they are hearing from God.

We are to recognize the voice of the Lord through wind, fire, or shaking. Sometimes we can simply feel or perceive the presence of the Lord in our midst. Most business people have been taught to operate according to "a hunch" or a "gut feeling." God says that He will guide us through His Holy Spirit, and He will teach and guide Christian business people and every believer in the way that they should go. This is how Jesus fulfilled His earthly ministry.

We are no longer left as orphans to do as we please with no parent to guide us. We have now been empowered by the Spirit of God, the Spirit of our Father, and we can tap into His wisdom from above, just as Jesus did in Luke 9:47.

Some have said that God speaks in only one way. This is not true. Our God is not a God of retrogression; He is a God of progression. God speaks even more to His people today than He did in the past. He is speaking to people more, not less. God wants to communicate with us and have fellowship with us. Indeed, He desires intimacy with us.

God also speaks in different ways. As a business person, or a parent, he will speak to you in that language. God wants to give you strategies for your business, your family and your personal life. He is not limited by just "church or spiritual language."

Guidelines for Hearing God's Voice

Active Listening. Be an active listener, not a passive hearer. Listen with the intent to understand, and when you hear, obey. Think of how it is with natural parents and children. Sometimes a child can tell from the tone of his or her parents' voices what their mood is or if they are in trouble. At other times, it is the looks on the parents' faces that give them the indication of what is about to happen to them. Sometimes the child can avoid trouble if he or she is sensitive enough to sense the parents' emotions before they are fully expressed. This is a good example of what I call "active listening."

Prayer: Prayer is meant to be a dialogue, a conversation between God and us. When we are in a spirit of prayer, God will often speak to us, and we must take time to listen for His voice.

Scriptural Support. To be sure you are hearing God's voice, the words you hear must be consistent with the principles that are laid out clearly for us in the Bible. God does not contradict himself; neither is He an author of confusion. (See 1 Cor. 14:33.) Sometimes people speak forth "prophetic words" that emanate from their own hearts and minds. We see this taking place in Jeremiah 28 where the false prophet Hananiah gave a word that the people would be in bondage only two years; the true prophetic word of the Lord, however, came through Jeremiah who said that the captivity would last for seventy years. It will interest you to know that Hananiah did not live very long after giving that false prophecy!

Be Challenged by Faith. At times we sense peace in our hearts concerning what we believe the Lord is directing us to do. A prophetic word may challenge our faith, but we must always remember when we are challenged to act by faith, not by sight.

Record, read, and meditate on what you hear prophetically. Paul instructed Timothy to go back and take those prophetic words that had been given to him and strengthen himself through those words and the Word. Obviously, they did not have tape recorders in Paul's days, but they did have a way of recording their prophetic words.

1. Search for a witness to your prophetic words (from your spirit, not your flesh).

2. Wage a good warfare with your prophetic words.

3. Do nothing differently unless you are clearly and definitely directed to do so. In this way you can *wait* on the Lord until you get His *Word,* His *will* and His *way.* Many people receive the word of the Lord, but they do not wait to be shown the way to do it. They step forth to carry out the task outside of the timing of God. We must always be careful never to get ahead of God.

Be Aware of These Hindrances:

1. The three sources of temptation: the world, Satan, and self.
2. Mind-sets, traditions, religion, and blind spots.
3. Lack of knowledge with regard to how God speaks.

Practical Tips for Hearing God's Voice:

1. Set a definite time and, if you can, find a definite and specific place to commune with God.
2. Create a holy habit of being quiet and listening to God.
3. Do these things often.
4. Listen in the spiritual realm.
5. Eliminate distractions even though that will seem hard to do. Be deliberate, however, in your attempts to do so.
6. Form a habit of entering into and practicing the presence of God.
7. Take captive every thought which is not of God. (See 2 Cor. 10:5.)
8. Talk to God. Pray without ceasing, and get very specific with Him.
9. Ask God questions, and then be silent in order to hear from Him.
10. Stay open to creative ways that the Lord might have for you to solve problems and straighten out issues.
11. Take written notes, and record His words.

Prayer Hints That Are Unique to Business:

• Pray strategically; you must have a plan to specifically present before God in prayer.
• Have a prayer support team.
• Pray specifically about discernment and pray in tongues, for the Spirit comes and intercedes for us with groans that words cannot even express.
• Pray about relationships, networking, business contacts, and personal opportunities to help others.
• Keep a prayer journal which will enable you to keep track of how wonderfully God answers your prayers.

A Final Encouragement

You can hear God's voice in the *agora* as well as in the sanctuary. Piety doesn't ensure clarity in this, but surrender does.

God's voice...
• encourages and dispels discouragement, for the Word of the Lord comes to edify, exhort, and comfort.
• brings peace where there is confusion.
• gives understanding where there has been frustration.
• gives hope where there is despair.
• strengthens faith where there is fear and doubt.
• invites praise and thanksgiving to dispel murmuring and complaining.
• gives direction where there is indecision.

Move out. Go into the marketplace. Expand the Kingdom, and reach people with the Good News of Jesus Christ. Follow biblical principles, and you will discover that God will give you the boldness, creativity, resources, and people to do Marketplace Ministry.

There is a great opportunity for believers to go beyond their greatest personal goals or expectations. God the Father, the Son, and the Holy Spirit are all desirous of interacting with us. This is an overwhelming thought. They want to direct us through every area of creation.

I want to bless you with the ability to hear the voice of the Lord in whatever form He may speak. God is a God of blessings. It gives Him pleasure when we are obedient to Him by operating in His Word. Your blessing will overtake you. Be blessed in your daily walk with the Lord and take courage.

Marketplace Ministry Action Steps

1. Put into action the practical steps for learning to hear God's voice:

a. Set a definite time and, if you can, find a definite, specific place to commune with God.

b. Form a habit of entering into His presence. (By the way, habits usually take at least twenty-one days to develop.)

c. Create a holy habit of being quiet and listening to God.

d. Do these things often.

e. Listen in the spiritual realm.

f. Eliminate distractions, even though that will seem hard in this day and time. Be deliberate in your attempts to do so.

g. Take captive every thought which is not of God. (See 2 Cor. 10:5.)

h. Talk to God. Pray without ceasing, and get very specific with Him.

i. Ask God questions and then be silent in order to hear from Him.

j. Stay open to creative ways that the Lord might have for you to solve problems and straighten out issues.

2. Take the following prayer hints that are unique to business and make them personal for you:

• Pray strategically. You must have a plan to specifically present before God in prayer. Write out your plan.

• Have a prayer support team. What are their names? Do they know your plan?

• Pray specifically about discernment, and pray in tongues, for the Spirit comes and intercedes for us with groans that words cannot even express.

• Pray about relationships, networking, business contacts, and personal opportunities to help others. Write down what the Holy Spirit reveals about these things.

• Keep a prayer journal to enable you to keep track of how wonderfully God answers your prayers. *Just do it!*

CHAPTER 13

Love: The Marketplace Ministry Value!

THE BIBLE SAYS THAT WE CAN DO GREAT AND POWERFUL
EXPLOITS FOR GOD, BUT IF THEY ARE DONE WITH THE WRONG
MOTIVATION OR WITHOUT LOVE, THEY WILL NOT LAST.
(1 CORINTHIANS 13)

Jesus said that He and His father are always at work even to this very day. (See John 5:17.) God did not simply finish the creation and stop working. He is still at work on your behalf, doing everything according to His master plan. His presence covers the earth. God not only created the universe, He also destined that it be governed by His principles, through the Church, for the ultimate fulfillment of His purposes and plans. In other words, God himself is our model for these principles. I often say, "The anointing (gifting) may get you there, but it is God's principles that will keep you there." Remember, there is power in His principles. When we keep our focus on Him and learn from Him, we begin to be able to effectively live by His principles.

Let's take a moment now to review the principles for success in Marketplace Ministry which we have discussed in the preceding chapters. They have been presented in a progression that, if followed, will build the foundation for success: As you will see, there is a progression starting with receiving God's vision.

Vision: We must know God has a predestined plan for our lives and that He is able to release it through our vision, which is the vision He has given to us.

Planning: God operates through a master plan, and our plan should be part of His plan. Without a plan we are likely to miss our destiny.

Workmanship: When we have received God's vision, we must now begin by applying the principles of work or workmanship.

Stewardship: We must know how to manage the resources God has provided for us and realize our responsibility and accountability for using them in our sphere of influence.

Servanthood: We need to know how to serve, work with, and relate to each other in our everyday encounters, including our workplace.

Ethics and Integrity: We must be aware of our conduct and behavior, then apply it on a consistent basis and learn to build our spiritual house so that it will stand firmly upon the Rock.

Hearing God: We must know and recognize the voice of God, listen to Him, and obey His words to us.

We have also learned that God has provided His Word and the local church to help us to learn and apply these principles in our daily lives. We know that God first considers what our attitude toward these principles is in order to determine our faithfulness in little things and see if we can be put in charge of even more. As we glean through the Scriptures, we begin to see that our behavior is guided by how well we incorporate and apply these principles into our daily walk. As these principles become our core value system and the foundation for our ethics, we will begin to see them operating in every aspect of our lives. Jesus clearly explained this process in Matthew 25:21: "You have been faithful with a few things; I will put you in charge of many things" (NIV). The few things Jesus spoke of will be what we are called to deal with on a daily basis at home, at work, and in church. Our goal as Christians is that we would be found faithful at the Judgment Seat of Christ and hear God say to us, "Well done, good and faithful servant!"

The methodology and consistency of our work with others and how we use the resources God has provided for us is our "code of conduct." Our marketplace "policies and procedures manual" is the Bible. The perfect model for our work place attitude, which is to be one of servanthood, is the life and ministry of Jesus. In this chapter, we will deal with the values that underpin our marketplace ethics and our personal integrity.

Marketplace Ministry Values

The definition of "value" is: *to be worth, strong, to wield; the desirability or worth of a thing, intrinsic value of a thing.*

Values can be described as those foundational principles from which we make quality life decisions as guided by God's "plumb line." God's "plumb line" centers on the principles of His Word by which He has commanded us to live. To choose to live by these principles is wisdom.

The Apostle Paul explains the distinction between earthly wisdom (the wisdom of this age) and God's wisdom in 1 Corinthians 2:6-7:

> *However, we speak wisdom among those who are mature, yet not the wisdom of this age, nor of the rulers of this age, who are coming to nothing. But we speak the wisdom of God in a mystery, the hidden wisdom which God ordained before the ages for our glory.*

In this passage of Scripture, Paul explains that this wisdom is for the mature who have integrity and understand it is the only way to success in life. Paul goes on to say, "Eye has not seen, nor ear has heard, nor have entered into the heart of man the things God has prepared for those who love Him." God has revealed these things to us by His Spirit.

Many would like to be successful in their business, but they do not really understand that success comes through operating within God's value system. Understanding and operating in God's principles enables the mature individual to apprehend success by revealing the mysteries of enterprise and economics that have been available to mankind since before time to him or her.

You can jump, shout, and pray for miracles all you want, but the most important requirement of all is that you walk in the principles of God so you will be able to apprehend what He has for you in the marketplace. You may receive mercy and answers to your prayers, but to have sustained success without the peaks and valleys you must be able to say to God, "I will follow your principles, no matter what the cost to me may be."

Determine Your Values

The question we must ask ourselves at this point is: *Who determines my values and by what yardstick or code of conduct are they measured?* The answer will depend on which area of life you are addressing, whether *personal, family, sociological, organizational, business/work, professional, etc.* Each arena of life may have its own set of values with applicable codes of conducts as perceived from a given point of view. Even the Mafia and other crime organizations have their "codes of conduct," which are based on their own perceived "value systems."

The only values that last, though, are God's values which have been given to us through His principles, principles that are contained within His Word. God's "plumb line" must become the standard by which we measure all our values and how we determine our personal "code of conduct." If you own a business or are the CEO of a company with the responsibility for determining its policy and procedures, you must have your set values in place. If you do not have a conscious set of values, your company will invariably pick up the values of the worldly system. I have expressed this many times in helping entrepreneurs as they embark on their business ventures.

Values that are based upon biblical principles become our anchors in times of testing. We must always ask, "WWJD — *What Would Jesus Do?*" or "WWJS — *What Would Jesus Say?*" to come up with a biblical solution for any situation. We must stay conscious of the fact that everything we do must be based on a set value system. As Christians, these values need to be based on God's principles. We must consistently ask the Lord: "What is your solution to this problem? How do you want me to respond to that issue?"

Purpose and Values

Upholding God's values brings consistency and favor not only with God but also with man. The Bible tells us that "Jesus increased in wisdom and stature, and in favor with God and men" (Luke 2:52). John 1:14 tells us that "The Word became flesh and dwelt among us." As Jesus was the Word made flesh, we are called to be the flesh made the Word, thus demonstrating God's truth and grace.

Boundaries and Values

God's principles and value systems are meant to set safety boundaries to keep us out of trouble and to help us not miss the mark. God's unconditional love does not negate the boundaries that have been set by His value system. In the beginning, when God created man and woman and placed them in the Garden of Eden, He established boundaries that were actually a reflection of His value system. He told them to work and care for the Garden. They could eat from any tree in the Garden, except the Tree of the Knowledge of Good and Evil.

These limits or boundaries were necessary to establish standards of right and wrong for generations to come.

The Apostle Paul said that he would not have known what sin was except through the Law. (See Rom. 7:7.) If the Law had not delineated God's boundaries, life would have been governed by what felt good or by what each person thought was best. Because God is absolute, however, His laws and principles set the yardstick for proper living, while, at the same time, exposing sin.

In Ezekiel 47:12 the prophet records that there is a river flowing from the throne of God, and the trees that grow by its water bear much fruit. This river is the grace of God that is flowing to mankind. Just as the trees that stay within the boundaries of the river bear much fruit, so must we stay within the standards and boundaries of God's principles in order to bear fruit in our lives. The trees that try to grow away from the river cannot bear fruit, and they have to struggle just to stay alive.

The Book of Psalms begins by laying out the boundaries and the pretext for the rest of the Psalms. (See Ps. 1-2.) The first ones are the boundaries for the individual and the second ones represent the boundaries of the Son who reigns over the nations.

The "blessed man" who is described in Psalm 1 is one who finds his delight:

> *... in the law of the Lord, and in His law he meditates day and night. He shall be like a tree planted by the rivers of water,*

that brings forth its fruit in its season, whose leaf also shall not wither; and whatever he does shall prosper. (Ps. 1:3)

The Law of the Lord presents the principles that the Lord teaches us. In the New Testament, Jesus further defines God's boundaries in the Sermon on the Mount. (See Matt. 5:1-10.) He defines the Law in terms of heart attitudes and man's relationship with God and with one another. Often the boundaries Jesus set were higher than those of the Law, and they required more personal accountability both to God and to others. Man would no longer be judged by the letter of the Law, but on his thoughts, his motives, and the state of his heart.

Jesus taught that the mouth speaks out of the heart. It's not what goes into a person that breaks the Law; it's what comes out of him or her. Jesus came to work on our hearts and to take us to a higher level of values.

The Golden Rule—a Bedrock Value for the Marketplace

Do for others what you would like them to do for you. This is a summary of all that is taught in the law and the prophets. (Matt. 7:12, NLT)

This is the Golden Rule. Our faith runs parallel to our behavior. In our teaching of business development courses through the Nehemiah School of Business, we try to keep the Golden Rule as fundamental as possible. We build from a simple foundational blueprint or diagram. The diagram describes Faith as our mission or driving force; Hope as the God-given vision and Love as the motivation or purpose.

Faith is the revelation or substance of things that are accomplished as an organization moves toward the hope of its God-given vision for existence or purpose. However, the key standard or litmus test is always found in the answer to the question, "Why?" Why are we doing this, or more specifically what is our motivation? Is love motivating us? If it is, it will last. This is the reason that of these three core values—faith, hope and love—love is the greatest! (See 1 Cor. 13:13.) This is because love represents the motivation upon which we build our entire value system.

How do we apply this in Marketplace Ministry? As we begin to apply self-discipline to God's boundaries and values in our everyday lives, we start to live out the Golden Rule. We begin to change the way we look at business, money, competition, customers, employees, employers, suppliers, and everything else involved in daily life. We begin to really do to others as we want them to do to us. This is opposite to the world's "golden rule," which says, "Do unto others before they can do it to you." Also, we often hear the statement, "He who has the gold makes the rules."

The Bible talks about the importance of *faith, hope, and love.* Faith is the active ingredient in our behavior that determines what we do and how we respond towards hope in order to fulfill our destiny. If we do not have love operating in our lives, if we cannot do unto others as we want them to do unto us, then we have the wrong motivation in our hearts. This means that we may need "a heart transplant." This is what Jesus was referring to when He said that from the heart a man speaks. The Apostle Paul also writes that you can have all the good deeds in the world but if you don't have love, you have nothing. (See 1 Cor. 13:1-3.)

The Motivating Value—Love!

The key motivation for all we do must be love. Jesus said the Good Samaritan fulfilled the Law by loving his neighbor regardless of who he was or where he came from. It was not a case of "What's in it for me?" or "I'll do this for you if you do this for me." There was no trade-off in this example of "loving your neighbor as yourself." Love of this caliber is at the heart of the value system God wants for us to live in and use at all times.

When we do business within this kind of value system, we are operating in faith, because we are trusting God. As we do so, we can confidently pray, "God, my responsibility is to you so you can be responsible for me. I am going to keep your principles and operate within your value system, no matter what happens around me or to me."

The Core of the Jabez Prayer

When Bruce Wilkinson's best-selling book on *The Prayer of Jabez* was released, many Christians began using this prayer as a kind of mantra, believing it would help them succeed or prosper. Unfortunately, many missed an essential truth that is contained within this prayer. Jabez sought for God to keep him with his boundaries so that he would not hurt others. In other words, love became the boundary for his daily life.

> *And Jabez called on the God of Israel saying, "Oh, that You would bless me indeed, and enlarge my territory, that Your hand would be with me, and that You would keep me from evil, that I may not cause pain!" So God granted him what he requested. (1 Chron. 4:10)*

Some time ago, a successful corporate consultant friend of mine, Gene Swindoll, wrote a small book entitled, *Jabez, Inc.*, which interprets the prayer of Jabez from a corporate perspective.

We can expect blessing and increase in the marketplace when all we do and say is within the eternal value of love. Henry Drummond was a scientist and an educator who understood love as a value. In *The Greatest Thing in the World* he wrote, "You will find, as you look back upon your life, that the moments when you have truly lived are the moments when you have done things in the spirit of love."

Jesus teaches us some important facets of this principle in Matthew 5:39-42:

If someone strikes you on the right cheek, turn to him the other also. And if someone wants to sue you for your tunic, let him have your cloak as well. If someone forces you to go one mile, go with him two miles. Give to the one who asks you, and do not turn away from the one who wants to borrow from you. (NIV)

This is a basic lesson in commerce and provides us with the answer to the question, "How do I become wealthy when I don't have any money?" Jesus said all you do is give more of yourself than is required of you. Do all you can in every circumstance, just as Joseph did in his marketplace.

In every relationship, business situation, or transaction, we must be willing to do whatever it takes to complete what God is calling us to do. We must be willing to go beyond the ordinary to accomplish the extraordinary until doing so becomes natural to us. As new creations in Christ Jesus, we must no longer regard others from a worldly point of view. The old has passed away and the new has begun, in us and through us. We have been given the ministry of reconciliation by God himself. (See 2 Cor. 5:18-20). Hence, irrespective of another's love, appreciation, or esteem of us, we must love him or her through Christ.

Even in the secular realm, businesses today are developing and operating with core values. As simple as it may sound, Marketplace Ministry finds its foundational core values in three simple words: *faith, hope, and love...and the greatest of these is love.*

When Jesus was asked the question about which is the greatest commandment in the Law, He answered:

"You shall love the LORD your God with all your heart, with all your soul, and with all your mind." This is the first and great commandment. And the second is like it: "You shall

love your neighbor as yourself.'" On these two commandments hang all the Law and the Prophets (Matt. 22:37-40).

So all the values and ethics upon which we are to build our core values hang on this great commandment.

Paul summed up all his teaching on gifts in the Church and the whole of the Law with one word—love. (See 1 Cor. 13.) Yes, we begin with faith in God through Christ. Yes, the Holy Spirit fills us with hope so that we do not live in despair, depression, or discouragement. But ultimately, what Marketplace Ministry brings to the world that no other value system can equal is simply God's love in Christ for which the Christian offers no apology!

And hope does not disappoint us, because God has poured out his love into our hearts by the Holy Spirit, whom he has given us. You see, at just the right time, when we were still powerless, Christ died for the ungodly. Very rarely will anyone die for a righteous man, though for a good man someone might possibly dare to die. But God demonstrates his own love for us in this: While we were still sinners, Christ died for us. (Rom. 5:5-8, NIV)

Marketplace Ministry Action Steps

1.   Read this statement which was expressed at the beginning of this chapter:
"These limits or boundaries were necessary to establish a standard of right and wrong for all generations. "

2.   Now read Romans 7:7.

3.   Fill in the blanks with your name:

If the law had not shown _____ God's boundary, _____life would have been given over to what felt good to _____ or what _____ thought was best.

4.   Describe how important understanding God's principles and values are to you and to the next generation.

5.   What Marketplace Ministry brings to the world that no other value system can equal is _____, for which the Christian offers no apology!

6.   Are you a Christian? _____

7.   Are you bringing God's values into the marketplace where God has called you to be? _____

8.   What do you need to change in order to better accomplish this mission?

CHAPTER 14

Putting It All Together in Marketplace Ministry

To create a business is to create a value system. If you have not done so, I recommend that you read, *In Search of Excellence.* In this book, Dr. Tom Peters basically puts together his conclusions on what made particular businesses and people successful. He synthesized from his research that what made each one successful was the basic philosophy of good common sense, which is based upon solid values. Not only did they understand the values, but they practiced them. Many people are surprised to discover that most companies have not operated that way and some even "cook" their books.

Another best-selling business book is *Good to Great* by Jim Collins. It also studies the habits and attributes of successful organizations.

The United States is hated in some regions of the world because of the kinds of businesses we have created in the name of free speech and free enterprise. In addition to the good we have done as the most productive nation in history, we have also been productive in negative areas and have sold and propagated pornography, gambling, and other detrimental habits all over the world. Obviously, many countries are not happy about this exploitation or the "ME-isms" we promote in the name of *capitalism.*

Let's learn from the successes and mistakes of others. Your organization will crumble if the foundation is not based on the right set of values. However, if you build your family, your company, and your life on the right values, they will not fall in times of trouble or, as Jesus said, when the winds and storms come, they will stand.

For example, before mission statements became popular, Sears and Roebuck came up with this motto, "Quality at a Good Price." This may seem simple in today's high-tech marketplace, but it clearly expressed their value system to the public. Sears was also the first company to come up with the slogan, "I guarantee it."

This is a common phrase in the marketplace today where consumers do not have the time to read all the fine print that is found in written guarantees. The guarantee, however, is only as good as the values that are behind it.

Other companies have since followed this example by displaying their values to appeal to the public in order to gain their business and their trust. The Caterpillar Company, for example, offers twenty-four-hour customer service anywhere in the world. They have stated that if you have a breakdown, no matter where you are in the world, they will be there to assist you within twenty-four hours. And they keep their word! People buy Caterpillar machinery simply because of this added value. When we do what is right, and keep our word, being good stewards of that which God has given us, our businesses and our lives will flourish.

A company that is built on biblical principles must have a strong mission statement and a strong code of ethics. As you begin to develop your own set of values, take a serious look at the following inappropriate statements and business practices and determine to avoid them at all costs:
- It is not wrong if you don't get caught.
- Cheating on your income tax is not wrong because the government spends money unwisely anyway. How about your

expense accounts? Is it okay to manipulate them for the sake of a good business image?

• Have an overbearing non-compete clause.

• In secular business, briberies or under-the-table payments are a big problem. This is particularly true when dealing with other countries where such practices are considered the norm. These may be spoken or unspoken agreements.

A Driving Force in Marketplace Ministry

Years ago there was a merger between American Express and Fireman's Fund Company. American Express was a very aggressive and profit-driven company that was gaining all types of acquisitions. Fireman's Fund was a conservative, highly valued company with strong assets. The fundamental problem with this merger was there was a big difference between the cultures of the two companies. The Fireman's Fund had the largest Human Resource Department of any company of its size; American Express had the smallest. At Fireman's, everything was based on customer satisfaction, while American Express was built on cash flow. This culture clash was so extreme that they had to split up after three years.

What drives your company? It pays to know where your customers place their values. We all know that McDonald's began by placing a high value on cleanliness. When Ray Krock started the McDonald's franchise, he first looked at where his target customers placed their values. He discovered that cleanliness, timeliness, and something designed for the children were all very important to his prospective market. So he developed his company values around those three important personal values. We know how successful he was, because McDonald's is a favorite spot and highly recognized by most kids and adults today.

ASA is a Software company that is based in North Carolina. It provides outstanding benefits for its employees. They offer flextime, have on premises medical services, nurseries, and schools for their children. They also have a private golf course for their employees, among other valuable benefits. Their turnover since the company began remains at less than 2 percent, and they have never downsized. The company has enjoyed so much stability and profitability because of their value system. After their company was highlighted on the "60 Minutes" TV program, they received 15,000 applications. People want to work where they are valued by their employer. This is a company that was built on trust. Because of the trust that was established in the beginning they can operate on this basis. Many companies would like to have this type of environment, but do not know how to build the foundational structure that is required to do so.

The 1960's focus on the separation of Church, State, and Business has caused much confusion in the work place. This "movement" has caused godly ethics founded on biblical principles to be denigrated in the work place. But God is to be Lord over all things, and we, the Church, are to be agents of change in the whole world: the church, government, and business.

Marketplace Ministry in Education

Consider the educational system and the problems we have in this country with productivity. A recent survey revealed that 60 percent of the students interviewed said they would cheat on their exams if they could do so without getting caught.

Public schools had prayer for nearly 200 years before the Supreme Court ruled that state-mandated class prayers were unconstitutional. Former Secretary of Education William Bennett revealed that between 1960 and 1990 there was a steady moral decline in our society. During this period the number of divorces doubled, teenage pregnancy went up 200 percent, teen suicide increased 300 percent, child abuse reached an all-time high, violent crime went up 500 percent, and abortion increased 1000 percent. Morals must be taught and they cannot be taught properly without godly principles as the core values of the education system. Most strong moral values stem from such biblically based truths as the Ten Commandments and the Golden Rule. There is a strong correlation between the expulsion of prayer from our schools and the decline in morality.

When we took prayer out of our schools, morality declined, SAT scores dropped, and these scores continue to drop even today. The government has become the watchdog, but who is watching the government? It seems the government has left behind the foundational structure that made this nation great.

In the same way we are confronted with a lack of ethics in the Church. There are real-life examples in the Old Testament that give us insights with regard to how to respond to the temptations of our human nature:

Elisha's Servant: In 2 Kings 5:22, Gehazi tried to receive an illegal honorarium from Naaman, the army general who came to Elisha with all kinds of gifts, because he wanted to be healed of leprosy. The Prophet Elisha refused the gifts to avoid any conflict of interest, but his servant Gehazi deceitfully accepted them, bringing a curse of leprosy upon himself. Elisha had character and values that were quite different from those of his servant.

The examples of Samuel and Samson: The difference between Samuel and Samson was clearly evident in their character and values. Samson did not have a good set of values and ethics, because he lacked character. As a result, he lost the opportunity and anointing to deliver Israel from all its troubles. After being physically blinded, he was finally able to see what his bad judgment and lack of moral character had done. Once he repented, he was able to fulfill some of his calling from God. Samuel refused to compromise godly values even when King Saul threatened him. He stood firm, but Samson compromised.

Joseph. No matter where or in what circumstances he found himself, Joseph consistently exhibited excellence in his values and behavior. Notice that his values and ethics were based on the Word of God and not on the circumstances he faced. Even when he was imprisoned, he exhibited such high moral ethics, values, and integrity that he ended up managing the prison. He was definitely a man of excellence.

Daniel. There was so much jealousy toward Daniel that his enemies investigated him on his ethics, but they could find no fault in him.

Solomon. When Solomon was to build the Temple, he made an excellent business connection with King Hiram who was willing to work in accord with Solomon's perspective of money management and values. Solomon knew this was an indication of Hiram's level of integrity. Solomon only used workers with excellent skills, such as those from the city of Gebal (1 Kings 5:18). Later in life, Solomon abandoned godly values in order to please his pagan wives by building idolatrous temples. His compromise with the world began a downward spiral for Israel that ultimately resulted in national division, civil war, and exile.

Christians in the Marketplace Must Raise the Bar

Bishop Bill Hamon, successful author as well as Founder and President of Christian International, gives the following "10 M's" as an acid test of our character:

1. Manhood (or Womanhood)
2. Ministry
3. Message
4. Maturity
5. Marriage
6. Methods

7. Manners
8. Money
9. Morality
10. Motive

In making decisions, consider the following as your guidelines:

• Is it legal?
• Is it ethical?
• Is it in line with the Word of God?
• What is God saying about it right now?

When you carefully consider this sequence, you eliminate errors and avoid troubles in your business and personal life. We all need a set moral baseline as the foundation for our families, businesses, and relationships. Always remember the truth that is expressed in Psalm 11:3-7:

> *If the foundations are destroyed,*
> *What can the righteous do?*
>
> *The LORD is in His holy temple,*
> *The LORD's throne is in heaven;*
> *His eyes behold,*
> *His eyelids test the sons of men.*
> *The LORD tests the righteous,*
> *But the wicked and the one who loves violence*
> *His soul hates.*
> *Upon the wicked He will rain coals;*
> *Fire and brimstone and a burning wind*
> *Shall be the portion of their cup.*
>
> *For the LORD is righteous,*
> *He loves righteousness;*
> *His countenance beholds the upright.*

An action is honorable only if it pleases God and His delegated authorities. We are to demonstrate God's values in all circumstances and be consistent even when we seem to be vulnerable. Unbelievers and innocent children learn from us and may fall short of meeting God's standards in their lives as a result of watching us.

Therefore, Incorporate These Values into Your Marketplace Ministry:

1. HONESTY: We must learn to be honest. (See 1 John 1:5-6.)

2. INTEGRITY: Adherence to God's principles; not moving to the left or the right. (See Ps. 24:3-4.)

3. COMMITMENT: It is very important to stick to your God-given task until it is accomplished. (See 1 John 3:16-18.)

4. STEWARDSHIP: This quality must be demonstrated in all areas of our life. (See 1 Cor. 4:1.)

5. LOYALTY: Our first loyalty is to God. But how can we be loyal to the unseen God if we don't learn to be loyal to man, whom we see everyday? (See Josh. 1.)

6. SERVING: We must consistently serve God and others and be Good Samaritans. (See John 13:1-15 and Luke 10:25-37.)

7. FAIRNESS: We must do everything with moderation and well-balanced proportion. (See Acts 6.)

8. YOUR WORD MUST BE YOUR BOND: Follow the Golden Rule. (See Matt. 7:12 and Luke 6:31.)

Avoid These Common Pitfalls

Do not fall into the trap of thinking:
• Everybody does it.
• Nobody will know.
• It's the only way to get ahead.
• Compromise little by little.
• They owe it to me.
• It's a dog-eat-dog world.
• Well, I am just doing my job.
• I'm a businessman, not a theologian.
• The more money I make, the more I can give to the Kingdom of God.
• The end justifies the means.
• As long as we all agree, then whatever we do is right.
• Heaven helps those who help themselves.

Remember These Biblical Truths and Admonitions:

• Do not say, "I'll do to him as he has done to me; I'll pay that man back for what he did!" (See Prov. 24:29.)
• Bless those who persecute you. (See Rom. 12:14).
• Do not repay anyone evil for evil. (See Rom. 12:17.)
• Do not take revenge. (See Rom. 12:19.)
• If your enemy is hungry, feed him. (See Rom. 12: 20.)
• Do not be overcome by evil, but overcome evil with good. (See Rom. 12: 21.)

Receive the Benefits and Blessings of God

If you operate in the biblical principles that I've outlined in this book:
• Your relationship with God will improve.
• Your frustration and stress will disappear.

• In the marketplace, whether in your own company or your work place, people will recognize that your Christian talk and your Christian walk are the same.

• You and God together will be much more effective in accomplishing and fulfilling your future, your purpose, and the calling on your life.

Marketplace Ministry Action Steps

1.   Now it's time to put into practice what you have learned.

• List the biblical principles that should determine the core values of a Christian company. Write out the Scriptures that back each one up.

2.   As a Christian leader in your area of influence, do the following:

• Repent and change your thinking to line up with God's principles.

• Change your personal value system to be in accord with God's.

• Set up a godly personal code of conduct.

• Make sure that your word is your bond.

3.   Begin each day by asking God to reveal His priorities, His opportunities, and His purposes to you. Write down what He shows you.

4. At the end of each day, evaluate your day. Pray and ask God to multiply the good seed you have sown and to compensate for those areas in which you feel you may have fallen short.

About
the Author

Apostle Paul "Buddy" Crum, M.B.A., M.A.B.S., Ph.RD., CFP

D
r. W. Paul "Buddy" Crum, Jr. is a visionary leader and author with a heart to empower God's people in the marketplace. With a successful business background prior to becoming a pastor, Dr. Buddy Crum is uniquely qualified to help churches develop marketplace ministry that changes businesses, communities and ultimately, nations.

Business

Before being ordained as a minister with Christian International in 1986, Buddy enjoyed a successful career as a corporate executive, entrepreneur, and organization consultant. As president of the Charter Capital Corporation in the 1970's, he was responsible for acquiring and managing a real estate portfolio valued at over $100 million. He served as senior V.P. and director of marketing for Financial Services Corporations, a national financial services company headquartered in Atlanta, Georgia, with offices in 37 states. Prior to being sold to a Fortune 500 company, it was recognized as one of the largest and premier investment companies in the nation. In 1985, Dr. Crum founded Charter Management Consultants, a consulting firm specializing in helping entrepreneurs acquire capital through investment banking firms.

Education

W. Paul (Buddy) Crum is a Certified Financial Planner (CFP). He received his Bachelor of Science degree from the University of Georgia, Master of Business Administration from Brenau University in Gainesville, Georgia, and his Doctorate of Religious Philosophy from Logos Graduate School. He also has a Master of Arts degree in Biblical Studies from Christian International Bible College and currently serves on the Board of Governor of Christian International.

Ministry

In 1986, he was ordained a minister with Christian International. In 1990, he became co-senior pastor of Life Center Family Church and director of Life Center Ministries, Inc., located in Dunwoody, Georgia. Along with his wife, Dr. Mary Crum, Dr. Crum helps church and business leaders discover their gifts of the spirit and destiny callings through individual consultations, workshops and conferences. He is an expert in the areas of team building, understanding personal purpose, empowering effective leaders, mentoring, developing potential and effective communication. Dr. Crum is president of Marketplace Alliance Group. He is a founding member of Christian International Business Network and founder of the Life Center Business Council, Life Center Business Cultivator and the International Christian Marketplace Alliance.

He has authored several books, including Spiritual Principles of Money, Pressing on with Joy, Turning Your Regrets into Remembrances, and The Future is Now – Breaking the Status Quo. He serves on the Board of Governors of Christian International Ministries and is a member of the Board of Directors for Christian International Business Network. As president of the Marketplace Alliance Group, he now devotes most of his time empowering churches and business leaders for marketplace ministry.

Life Center Ministries, Inc.
2690 Mt. Vernon Road
Dunwoody, GA 30338
770.399.0660
www.lifecenter.org